1999

Gardencycle™

A GARDENER'S DAY BOOK

CERTIFIED ORGANIC

Seeds *of* Change

Goodness from the ground up™

1999

Gardencycle™

SEEDS OF CHANGE™

COMPILED BY

Howard-Yana Shapiro, Ph.D., and John Harrisson

PHOTOGRAPHY BY

Scott Vlaun and Howard-Yana Shapiro, Ph.D.

TEN SPEED PRESS
BERKELEY, CALIFORNIA

Ten Speed Press
P.O. Box 7123
Berkeley, California 94707
www.tenspeed.com

Distributed in Australia by Simon and Schuster Australia, in
Canada by Ten Speed Press Canada, in New Zealand by Tandem
Press, in South Africa by Real Books, in Southeast Asia by
Berkeley Books, and in the United Kingdom and Europe by
Airlift Books.

Cover Design by Susan Caldwell
Interior Design by Susan Caldwell

First Printing, 1998
Printed in Singapore

1 2 3 4 5 6 7 8 9 10 – 02 01 00 99 98

This Day Book has been designed with a special breed in mind–the Gardener. It is meant to be a practical day-to-day record and a source of helpful information, documenting all the important aspects of your garden from design and preparation, to planting and growing, to harvesting and seed-saving. The purpose of this Day Book is also to provide a format for longer-term record keeping that will prove invaluable year after year. We hope *Gardencycle* will inspire you to roll up your sleeves and exercise your green thumb.

There are few activities in which it is so important to keep an accurate log of the days, weeks, and seasons, as it is in gardening. Any expert will tell you that the main keys to gardening success are to keep good records and to use that information. Knowing nature's patterns and cycles helps develop a better understanding and respect that will assist every gardener in cultivating a more beautiful and abundant garden. None of us accurately remembers the previous year's specific daily weather activity. We may well recall an early frost, a heavy snowfall, or a prolonged drought. But three years from now, will one be able to pinpoint these dates? Use *Gardencycle* to note your first and last frost dates, rainfall, planting, and harvest dates. You can compile daily weather information using the data boxes that appear below each day on the calendar. The data boxes (see legend on page 9) help you keep track of high and low temperatures, wind speed and direction, precipitation, and general weather conditions. This type of data can be crucial for identifying weather trends and maximizing results in the garden.

As the article on pages 12-13 details, the type of elementary record keeping gathered in *Gardencycle* involves simple observation of one's local area. Mastering this basic gardening skill leads to a better appreciation of natural patterns, which in turn produces superior, informed decisions about the design and management of one's garden. This is the beginning of a garden of paradise for each of us. In following years, you will be able to refer to this archive of information to repeat your successes and avoid the disappointments.

The format of *Gardencycle* is the result of years of record keeping by the individual gardeners who make up our team at *Seeds of Change*–not only on our research farms but also in our own gardens and backyards. It represents a synthesis of what works best for us, and what we like to keep track of during the year. In this endeavor, we step purposefully but humbly in the footsteps of those who have gone before us.

Countless cultures and civilizations preceding our own used both simple and incredibly complex systems to keep detailed records to sustain and develop the knowledge necessary for survival. Societies throughout the world used natural and man-made structures and equipment to observe and accurately document the passing of equinoxes, the shortest and longest days of the year, the advent of the planting season, and the harvest. The sun, stars, constellations, and planets were the guides.

Overlooking the fertile Oaxaca valley in southern Mexico, the elaborate Zapotec city of Monte Albán contains designs that replicate the position of the constellations and stars, indicating when the fields must be plowed, prepared, and planted. Ancient stone and wooden henges in Britain and Ireland were used by Druids to ascertain similar solar and astral calendrical data. In the Andean mountains and the arid badlands of the North American Southwest, elaborate carvings and apertures were fashioned in rocks and caves for the same purpose. Mayan observatories, Incan temples, and the pyramids of ancient Egypt were located and oriented to the position of the sun, moon, and stars, so that important dates could be recognized. Similar means and constructions have occurred around the globe, spanning the millennia.

Following in this tradition, *Gardencycle* incorporates astronomical information from the *Stella☆Natura* calendar, an annual publication of the Bio-Dynamic Farming and Gardening Association that provides practical advice to gardeners on how the various cosmic rhythms and events affect plant growth. We asked Sherry Wildfeuer, editor of *Stella☆Natura*,

to elaborate on the origins of this information and how it can be applied.

How can a contemporary gardener and thinker who has imbibed a materialistic education from childhood understand the idea that plant growth is related to cosmic rhythms?

This dilemma was addressed by Rudolf Steiner, Austrian philosopher and seer, who extended conventional science by integrating clear thinking with precise observation of sense-preceptible and spiritual phenomena. In 1924, Steiner gave a series of lectures in response to questions brought by farmers who noticed even then a deterioration in seed quality and animal fertility. This became the basis of the biodynamic movement.

The first principle he introduced was that we must broaden our perspective to include the whole universe as relevant to the life of nature. The light from the sun, moon, planets, and stars reaches the plants in regular rhythms, contributing to their life, growth, and form. By understanding the gesture and effect of each particular rhythm, we can time our ground preparation, sowing, cultivating, and harvesting to the advantage of the crops that we are raising.

For example, the few days preceding the full moon are the most stimulating for the germination of seeds. Plants grown from seeds that were sown on days of perigee, nodes, or eclipses will tend to be weak and vulnerable to fungus and pest attack. The moon acts as a kind of gate as it passes in front of the twelve constellations of the zodiac, opening the way for the influences of the four elements (earth, water, air, and fire) to enhance the root, leaf, flower, or fruit of plants that are sown and cultivated on those days.

The most notable research in this field has been done by a German farmer named Maria Thun, who publishes an agricultural calendar. Her research has shown that plants are receptive to the moon's passage through the uneven astronomical constellations of the zodiac. (The Stella✶Natura *calendar uses this information rather than the tropical signs used in popular astrology).*

In America, the Stella*Natura calendar makes these rhythms available, with practical advice for gardeners and farmers. Excerpts from the charts of Stella✶Natura *have been included in Gardencycle to indicate favorable times for sowing roots (such as carrots and potatoes), leafy vegetables (such as lettuce and kale), flowers (such as sunflowers and chamomile), and fruits and seeds (such as tomatoes, squash, beans, and wheat). Those times not favorable for sowing and planting are indicated by blank space in the calendar. The astronomical events are more fully explained, and their influences elaborated, in* Stella✶Natura, *which makes a great companion to this volume, as an introduction to biodynamics.*

It cannot be emphasized strongly enough that these indications are by no means intended to replace the gardener's own sense of timing or common sense. They are offered as information to consider when planning the timing of gardening activities for those who wish to be aware of the more subtle influences active in our gardens.

Working with cosmic rhythms is only one aspect of biodynamic gardening. I hope it will stimulate your interest to explore its scope more fully.

To order *Stella✶Natura*, contact The Bio-Dynamic Association, P.O. Box 550, Kimberton, PA 19442, or call 1.800.516.7797.

The material from the *Stella✶Natura* is one important aspect of the concept of the *cycle of the seasons* in the garden. In most locations, this cycle begins with dormancy and emerges gradually into regeneration and the intensity of activity, color, abundance, and harvest, and then once more winding down to a time of quiet. *Gardencycle* aims to establish a reference point from which the patterns of the year can be observed and recorded. As the Song of Solomon in the Old Testament records:

> To everything there is a season,
> and a time to every purpose under the Heaven.
> A time to be born, and a time to die; a time to plant,
> and a time to pluck up that which is planted;
> A time to kill, and a time to heal;
> a time to break down, and a time to build up;
> A time to weep, and a time to laugh;
> a time to mourn, and a time to dance...

We urge you, whenever and wherever you can, to take the time to both laugh and dance, to cultivate your garden of paradise, and along the way to learn from your observations and notes that you keep day by day, season by season, and year by year in your *Gardencycle*.

THE STAFF OF SEEDS OF CHANGE

NOTE ON GARDENCYCLE

INFORMATION DERIVED FROM

STELLA ☆ NATURA:

The information throughout the calendar is based on U.S. Eastern Standard Time (5 hours behind Greenwich Mean Time). Information given compensates for Daylight Saving Time, which begins on the first Sunday in April and ends on the last Sunday in October. Those living in other time zones of the United States should therefore allow for the time difference with Eastern Standard Time, and likewise for countries other than the United States.

LEGEND

The terms ROOT, LEAF, FLOWER, *and* FRUIT *appear in the calendar when the moon's presence in a constellation is beneficial to that part of the plant. Factor this information into your decisions about when to sow different kinds of plants.*

| ROOT | LEAF | FLOWER | FRUIT |

TEMPERATURE

MAX./MIN. _78/54_ °F /°C

PRECIPITATION

CONDITIONS

WIND

N NE (E) SE S SW W NW N

◗ ~ *Rain or snow*

◗ ~ *Frequent showers*

△ ~ *Occasional showers/drizzle*

△ ~ *No precipitation*

☼ ~ *Mostly sunny*

◑ ~ *Partly cloudy*

● ~ *Mostly cloudy*

Step outside your door and employ the fundamental tool of gardening–observation. Notice where the prevailing winds come from, where the water falls, how it runs off your land, your city rooftop, or your suburban lot. Where is there shelter and shade? How much sunlight do you receive? How do these climatic and environmental factors affect what you can grow? When you become familiar with the natural patterns that affect your location through observation, you can begin to work with them to your advantage and turn them into resources.

Australian Bill Mollison, who coined the term *Permaculture* (*perma*nent agri*culture*) and has pioneered this innovative system of sustainable gardening and agriculture since the late 1970s, has based his theories and their practical application on observation and natural patterns. Mollison provides examples of how to interpret observations: "Reading the landscape is a matter of looking for *landscape indicators*. Vegetation in particular provides information about soil fertility, availability of moisture, and microclimate. Rushes, for example, indicate boggy soils or seepages; dandelions and blueberries indicate acid soils; and docks suggest compacted or clayey soils. Large trees growing in dry regions indicate a source of deep water. An abundance of thorny or unpalatable

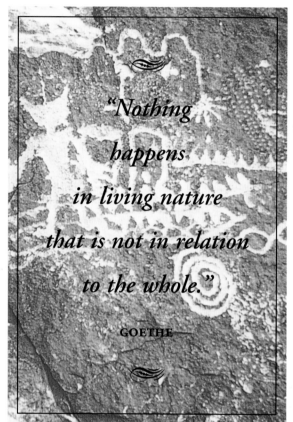

"Nothing happens in living nature that is not in relation to the whole."

GOETHE

weed species (such as thistles) indicates overgrazing or land mismanagement, and erosion gullies and compacted pathways will give you confirmation of this. A plant flowering and fruiting earlier than others of the same species indicates an advantageous microclimatic condition, and trees growing with most of their branches on one side indicate the direction of strong prevailing winds."

Climatic conditions affecting your garden are a primary determinant of vegetation and of gardening strategies. Observing how general weather trends progress through the seasons to affect your microclimate allows you to design your garden or site to buffer extremes of climate. Working with nature's design is crucial, and it can have tremendous benefit for your plantings. The following climatic factors are among those that can be observed to your great potential benefit:

SUNLIGHT.

In triggering the chemical process of photosynthesis, sunlight provides the essential source of energy for plants. Noting areas of full sunlight and shade will affect which plants are located in which area of the garden, and in what relationship to structures. Dark objects (including man-made structures, vegetation, and mulch) tend to absorb light while light-colored ones, including water, reflect it. Using a dark mulch in winter or spring can help warm and insulate the ground, for example. Conversely, plants with light-colored leaves or light-colored mulch (such as straw) can be used to reflect sunlight towards nearby plants located in darker places. Reflecting sunlight can also be beneficial in minimizing water evaporation. In general, creating suntraps in the garden can help growth, while reflected sunlight can be used for heating and as a source of indirect light.

Creating shade with trees, plants, and structures can be an important aspect of garden design, as shade protects plants from intense sunlight. You can predict the shading effect of planting certain trees or plants by holding a pole or some object of similar size in the sunlight and observing how and where the shadow falls. Remember the time of year and observe the path of the sun, and take these factors into account.

RAINFALL AND WATER.

Observing trends in rainfall and runoff in your garden or on your site enables you to design a system to retain as much water as possible, whether in the soil, in vegetation, or in a storage system. The idea is to reuse water (including household "gray water") as advantageously and repeatedly as possible, particularly in drier climates. In doing so, you can create new and beneficial habitats which will also minimize soil erosion.

Knowledge of annual rainfall and seasonal rainfall trends can also help you determine the sustainability of your gardening practices and the type of plants appropriate for your site. Although most gardeners rely mainly on public water supplies or their own well water, the more rainfall you are able to harvest, store, and use on your site, the more sustainable your garden. All gardeners everywhere should harvest water.

WIND.

Excessive winds can be very destructive. Therefore, observing wind patterns will provide the information you need to determine where to plant wind-tolerant trees such as poplar, beech, sycamore, and willows as windbreaks to protect your plants and property. Hedges, shrubs, and fences can also be used to protect gardens, while glass cloches can be used for small plants or seedlings. Windbreaks should be used to protect the garden not just from prevailing winds but also from other directions that may bring cold weather and wind chills that can be even more damaging to vegetation.

Observing or researching patterns of wind direction and strength allows you to take steps to design your garden, house, and other structures in such a way that the effect of the wind is minimized. Accurate off-site data on wind can be obtained from local weather stations and newspapers, and on-site information can be gained from your neighbors, especially if they happen to be the observant type. However, the shape of existing trees provides the most reliable evidence of wind direction and strength. Put up a colorful windsock, some flags, and some wind chimes so you can see the air currents and listen to the wind.

MICROCLIMATE FACTORS.

Observing and interpreting climatic differences between your particular location and your area or region in general can be pivotal in garden design. Understanding your particular microclimate can help you to modify its negative aspects or enhance its positive aspects. For example, by creating suntraps and diverting cold air with natural vegetation, trellises, or walls, you can extend the growing season and minimize frosts. Observing the first and last frost dates and collecting information from past years will help you accurately define your particular growing season.

Observing the topography of your site is particularly important and will help make certain gardening decisions simple. For example, some plants prefer a sunny southern aspect, while others thrive in a northern or eastern exposure. Likewise, the slope of the ground affects its temperature, water flow and retention, and wind flow. Creating windbreaks and contouring the land to control water and prevent erosion are examples of applying such observations.

Universal pattern is the template into which we fit the information assembled from observation and research; it reveals how all the component elements in and around the garden are stitched together and interwoven. Understanding basic patterns teaches us much about nature and natural phenomena. Australian master gardener and founder of Permaculture, Bill Mollison, observes, "In a natural landscape, each element is part of the greater whole, a sophisticated and intricate web of connections and energy flows. If we attempt to create landscapes using a strictly objective viewpoint, we will produce awkward and dysfunctional designs because all living systems are more than just a sum of their parts."

Viewing landscapes in terms of pattern rather than unconnected parts is one of the most difficult and complex aspects of garden design. While some people are adept at recognizing and "reading" patterns, most of us are not, though we could learn by practice. Mollison suggests that with the advent of writing, symbols (letters of the alphabet) have replaced a former connection to reality and experience, and as a result we have become divorced from a patterns of nature.

Day to day, we are surrounded by a complex array of shapes and forms, and many of the most basic patterns can be observed in quite distinct contexts. For example, wave patterns can be seen in water, sand dune formations, and in fossils; curled "jet" shapes are common to lava flows, rivers in flood, fungi, and ferns. Galaxy-type spirals can be observed in the seed head patterns of sunflowers and in whirlpools; overlapping spirals form leaf shapes that are also seen in flower petals, pine cones, and pineapples. Netlike matrices occur in honeycombs, dried mud cracks, tree bark, inside bones, and in basalt columns (such as the Giant's Causeway in Northern Ireland). What most of these different patterns have in common is that they are caused by flow or growth. They can all be seen as consequences of fractal geometrics.

Another type of pattern—dendritic or treelike branching—occurs in stream and river formations, blood vessels, and "fingers" of atmospheric lightning, as well as in trees, which branch out successively as they grow upward. A set pattern of branching and consistent ratios occur in each of these different contexts. In fact, all of these patterns occur universally, wherever in the world you choose to look, making landscape design decisions much easier and more predictable.

THE EDGE EFFECT ~ All patterns have boundaries and edges, and in nature, edges or interfaces that divide different media (water, air, land, or soil) or neighboring types of ecology or landscapes (such as forest and meadow, cropland and orchard, plain and marsh, desert and grassland, mountain and valley) are areas of the richest environment and greatest ecological diversity and productivity. This is not only because resources from both ecologies are brought into play, maximizing diversity, but also because edges often support species unique to these margins. Edges attract debris and other materials that can be important to the micro-ecology of the location—garden borders and fences accumulate leaves or soil blown by the wind, for example, and the jetsam found on the beach at the high-water mark can include seeds, nuts,

EFFECT:

PATTERNS TO DESIGN THE GARDEN

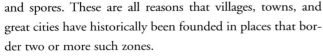

and spores. These are all reasons that villages, towns, and great cities have historically been founded in places that border two or more such zones.

You can use the pattern of edge in your garden by accentuating or expanding such areas or by creating them. For example, you can create small ponds and dams in open fields or yards, and given sufficient space, create islands in the water. You can introduce water margin plants such as rushes and waterlilies, and introduce aquaculture—fish and amphibians. By planting hedge-rows, orchards, or coppices of trees, you can create habitat as well as edge. You can create edge in an upward dimension in a flat garden by mounding earth and using contours not only for planting but as a windbreak or suntrap. Build a mound of earth and maximize its surface area by spiraling plants—herbs, for example—up and around it. This has the desirable net result of holding more plants than the same area of flat garden land. Planting can also take into account the edge between the sun and shade preferences of plants; in the case of herbs, the sunny, dry side is suitable for rosemary, thyme, and sage, while the shadier, moister side would be best for cilantro (coriander), mint, parsley, and chives.

Terraces, paths and garden borders, fences, and structures on the property can all be used to create edge. Another technique for providing more edge area is to create borders with wavy or crenelated edges; a pond in a rounded star shape, for example, has up to double the edge area of a perfectly circular pond occupying the same area. A trellis designed in a zigzag pattern provides greater growing area for vine crops or climbing plants compared to a straight-line trellis or fence occupying the same space. Planting seeds or seedlings in a triangular pattern (creating a hexagonal pattern on a larger scale) allows about thirty percent more plantings compared to a square matrix because there is less space between plants. This optimal density reduces the amount of weeds that can grow in the gap between plants.

A further method of maximizing edge is to grow parallel strips of quite different crops ("edge cropping"), an idea replicating patterns of coastal vegetation, where forest and plants border the beach. For example, rows of fruit trees, cover crops, vegetables, and sunflowers can be planted in a sequence allowing for shade, wind direction, etc. Even more productive are edge cropping rows planted in a zigzag or wavy design, as more plants can be accommodated in the same area compared to a linear design. Some gardeners, such as Dr. Howard-Yana Shapiro, Director of Agriculture at Seeds of Change, favor "rooms" of crops: a square patch of beans or cover crop, for example, surrounded by "walls" of corn, sorghum, or sunflowers. Such a patchwork quilt of patterning (called "tessellation" or tilelike) not only is visually pleasing but also encourages diversity and can be used to attract bees and other pollinators in a deliberate and beneficial pattern, or to create a buffer to cross-pollination. Isolated domains can be established this way to help maintain genetically pure lines; in this model, it is important to grow compatible crops or plants together.

MONDAY 28	TUESDAY 29	WEDNESDAY 30

Commit to recording weather information and your observations in this GARDENCYCLE diary throughout the year.

Begin to plan your garden layout for the coming year. Remember to rotate your crops and maximize diversity.

JANUARY

M	T	W	T	F	S	S
				I	2	3
4	5	6	7	8	9	10
II	12	13	14	15	16	17
18	19	20	21	22	23	24
25	26	27	28	29	30	31

FLOWER

FLOWER

LEAF

LEAF

TEMPERATURE	TEMPERATURE	TEMPERATURE
MAX./MIN. _____ °F /°C	MAX./MIN. _____ °F /°C	MAX./MIN. _____ °F /°C
PRECIPITATION	PRECIPITATION	PRECIPITATION
CONDITIONS	CONDITIONS	CONDITIONS
WIND	WIND	WIND
N NE E SE S SW W NW	N NE E SE S SW W NW	N NE E SE S SW W NW

THURSDAY 31

FRIDAY 1

New Year's Day

SATURDAY 2

ROOT

LEAF

FLOWER

FLOWER

FRUIT

TEMPERATURE

MAX./MIN. _____ °F /°C

PRECIPITATION

CONDITIONS

WIND

N   NE   E   SE   S   SW   W   NW

SUNDAY 3

LEAF

TEMPERATURE

MAX./MIN. _____ °F /°C

PRECIPITATION

CONDITIONS

WIND

N   NE   E   SE   S   SW   W   NW

Thursday 31
TEMPERATURE

MAX./MIN. _____ °F /°C

PRECIPITATION

CONDITIONS

WIND

N   NE   E   SE   S   SW   W   NW

Friday 1
TEMPERATURE

MAX./MIN. _____ °F /°C

PRECIPITATION

CONDITIONS

WIND

N   NE   E   SE   S   SW   W   NW

Saturday 2
TEMPERATURE

MAX./MIN. _____ °F /°C

PRECIPITATION

CONDITIONS

WIND

N   NE   E   SE   S   SW   W   NW

*Ah!
when shall all men's good
Be each man's rule, and
universal peace
Lie like a shaft of light across
the land,
And like a lane of beams
athwart the sea,
Through all the circle of the
golden year?*

ALFRED, LORD TENNYSON

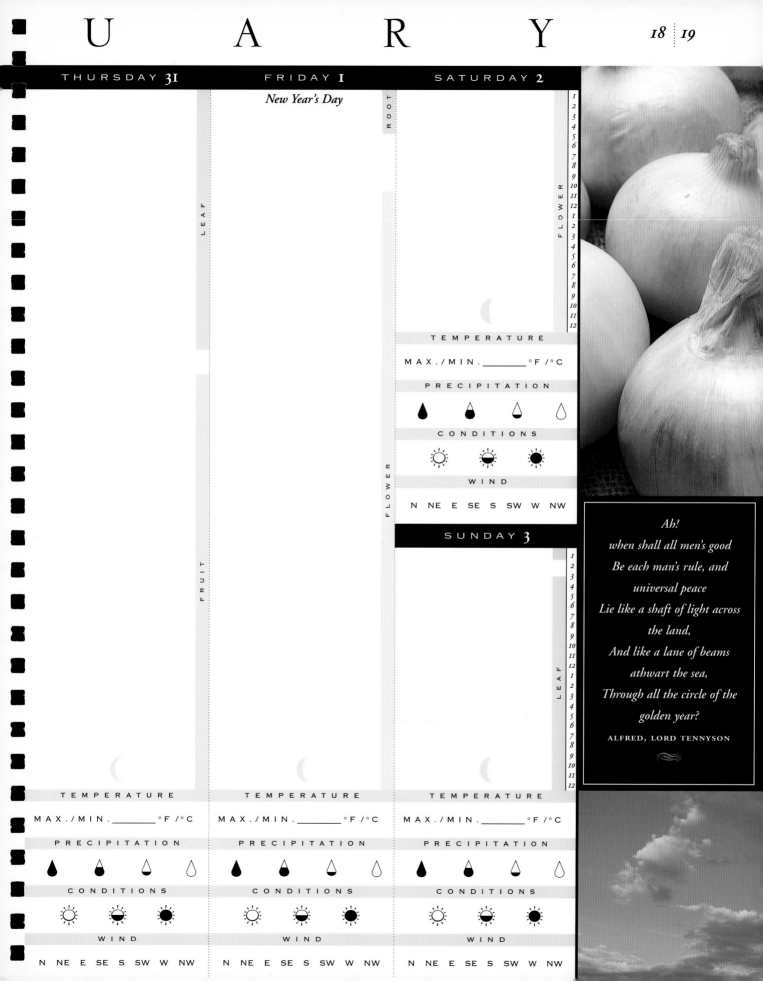

MONDAY 4

TUESDAY 5

WEDNESDAY 6

Recycle Christmas trees by pruning the branches and using them as mulch.

Join or start a local seed-savers group, or contact Seed Savers Exchange, a nonprofit organization dedicated to preserving diversity and endangered plants (see Resources, page 138).

LEAF

FRUIT

FRUIT

FRUIT

JANUARY

M	T	W	T	F	S	S
				I	*2*	*3*
4	*5*	*6*	*7*	*8*	*9*	*10*
II	*I2*	*I3*	*I4*	*I5*	*I6*	*I7*
I8	*I9*	*20*	*2I*	*22*	*23*	*24*
25	*26*	*27*	*28*	*29*	*30*	*3I*

I 2 3 4 5 6 7 8 9 I0 II I2 I 2 3 4 5 6 7 8 9 I0 II I2

TEMPERATURE

MAX./MIN. _____ °F /°C

PRECIPITATION

CONDITIONS

WIND

N NE E SE S SW W NW

TEMPERATURE

MAX./MIN. _____ °F /°C

PRECIPITATION

CONDITIONS

WIND

N NE E SE S SW W NW

TEMPERATURE

MAX./MIN. _____ °F /°C

PRECIPITATION

CONDITIONS

WIND

N NE E SE S SW W NW

THURSDAY 7   FRIDAY 8   SATURDAY 9

FRUIT

ROOT

ROOT

ROOT

1 2 3 4 5 6 7 8 9 10 11 12 1 2 3 4 5 6 7 8 9 10 11 12

TEMPERATURE

MAX. / MIN. _____ °F / °C

PRECIPITATION

CONDITIONS

WIND

N NE E SE S SW W NW

SUNDAY 10

ROOT

1 2 3 4 5 6 7 8 9 10 11 12 1 2 3 4 5 6 7 8 9 10 11 12

The frost performs its secret ministry
Unhelped by any wind.

SAMUEL TAYLOR COLERIDGE

Every mile is two in winter.

GEORGE HERBERT

(1651)

TEMPERATURE

MAX. / MIN. _____ °F / °C

PRECIPITATION

CONDITIONS

WIND

N NE E SE S SW W NW

TEMPERATURE

MAX. / MIN. _____ °F / °C

PRECIPITATION

CONDITIONS

WIND

N NE E SE S SW W NW

TEMPERATURE

MAX. / MIN. _____ °F / °C

PRECIPITATION

CONDITIONS

WIND

N NE E SE S SW W NW

MONDAY **11**   TUESDAY **12**   WEDNESDAY **13**

Read a book on preserving, drying, canning, and bottling garden produce, and factor what you learn into your plans for this year's harvest.

Make sure water does not collect and sit on any part of this year's food garden.

JANUARY

M	T	W	T	F	S	S
				1	2	3
4	5	6	7	8	9	10
11	12	13	14	15	16	17
18	19	20	21	22	23	24
25	26	27	28	29	30	31

1 2 3 4 5 6 7 8 9 10 11 12 1 2 3 4 5 6 7 8 9 10 11 12

FLOWER

FLOWER

LEAF

LEAF

TEMPERATURE

MAX./MIN. _____ °F /°C

PRECIPITATION

CONDITIONS

WIND

N NE E SE S SW W NW

TEMPERATURE

MAX./MIN. _____ °F /°C

PRECIPITATION

CONDITIONS

WIND

N NE E SE S SW W NW

TEMPERATURE

MAX./MIN. _____ °F /°C

PRECIPITATION

CONDITIONS

WIND

N NE E SE S SW W NW

THURSDAY 14

FRIDAY 15

SATURDAY 16

*I
2
3
4
5
6
7
8
9
10
11
12
I
2
3
4
5
6
7
8
9
10
11
12*

FRUIT

LEAF

FRUIT

TEMPERATURE

MAX./MIN._____°F /°C

PRECIPITATION

CONDITIONS

WIND

N NE E SE S SW W NW

SUNDAY 17

*I
2
3
4
5
6
7
8
9
10
11
12
I
2
3
4
5
6
7
8
9
10
11
12*

FRUIT

ROOT

*In the bleak midwinter
Frosty wind made moan,
Earth stood hard as iron,
Water like stone;
Snow had fallen, snow on snow,
Snow on snow,
In the bleak midwinter,
Long ago.*

CHRISTINA ROSSETTI

TEMPERATURE

MAX./MIN._____°F /°C

PRECIPITATION

CONDITIONS

WIND

N NE E SE S SW W NW

TEMPERATURE

MAX./MIN._____°F /°C

PRECIPITATION

CONDITIONS

WIND

N NE E SE S SW W NW

TEMPERATURE

MAX./MIN._____°F /°C

PRECIPITATION

CONDITIONS

WIND

N NE E SE S SW W NW

MONDAY 18   **TUESDAY 19**   **WEDNESDAY 20**

Martin Luther King Jr.'s
Birthday (Observed)

ROOT

ROOT

ROOT

FLOWER

FLOWER

*Research your local
microclimate thoroughly so
you can optimize the coming
planting and growing season.
Talk to neighbors,
contact the local Agriculture
Extension office, and
research weather records
at your local library.
Spend time in your garden
and consider how this
information can be used
to your advantage.*

JANUARY

M	T	W	T	F	S	S
			1	2	3	
4	5	6	7	8	9	10
11	12	13	14	15	16	17
18	19	20	21	22	23	24
25	26	27	28	29	30	31

TEMPERATURE

MAX./MIN. _____ °F /°C

PRECIPITATION

CONDITIONS

WIND

N NE E SE S SW W NW

TEMPERATURE

MAX./MIN. _____ °F /°C

PRECIPITATION

CONDITIONS

WIND

N NE E SE S SW W NW

TEMPERATURE

MAX./MIN. _____ °F /°C

PRECIPITATION

CONDITIONS

WIND

N NE E SE S SW W NW

THURSDAY 21

FRIDAY 22

SATURDAY 23

FLOWER

LEAF

LEAF

TEMPERATURE

MAX./MIN. _____ °F / °C

PRECIPITATION

CONDITIONS

WIND

N NE E SE S SW W NW

SUNDAY 24

FRUIT

LEAF

Blow, blow, thou winter wind,
Thou art not so unkind
As man's ingratitude
WILLIAM SHAKESPEARE

The trumpet of a prophecy!
O Wind,
If winter comes, can spring be
far behind?
PERCY BYSSHE SHELLEY

TEMPERATURE

MAX./MIN. _____ °F / °C

PRECIPITATION

CONDITIONS

WIND

N NE E SE S SW W NW

TEMPERATURE

MAX./MIN. _____ °F / °C

PRECIPITATION

CONDITIONS

WIND

N NE E SE S SW W NW

TEMPERATURE

MAX./MIN. _____ °F / °C

PRECIPITATION

CONDITIONS

WIND

N NE E SE S SW W NW

MONDAY 25 **TUESDAY 26** **WEDNESDAY 27**

Start saving recyclable household items like egg cartons, yogurt cartons, and plastic containers to start seeds in.

Make your own flats for your seeds and take the time to repair old ones.

JANUARY

M	T	W	T	F	S	S
			1	2	3
4	5	6	7	8	9	10
11	12	13	14	15	16	17
18	19	20	21	22	23	24
25	26	27	28	29	30	31

ROOT

FLOWER

ROOT

TEMPERATURE

MAX./MIN. _____ °F /°C

PRECIPITATION

CONDITIONS

WIND

N NE E SE S SW W NW

TEMPERATURE

MAX./MIN. _____ °F /°C

PRECIPITATION

CONDITIONS

WIND

N NE E SE S SW W NW

TEMPERATURE

MAX./MIN. _____ °F /°C

PRECIPITATION

CONDITIONS

WIND

N NE E SE S SW W NW

THURSDAY 28   **FRIDAY 29**   **SATURDAY 30**

ROOT

FLOWER

LEAF

1
2
3
4
5
6
7
8
9
10
11
12
1
2
3
4
5
6
7
8
9
10
11
12

FLOWER

TEMPERATURE

MAX./MIN. _____ °F / °C

PRECIPITATION

CONDITIONS

WIND

N NE E SE S SW W NW

SUNDAY 31

1
2
3
4
5
6
7
8
9
10
11
12

FLOWER

TEMPERATURE

MAX./MIN. _____ °F / °C

PRECIPITATION

CONDITIONS

WIND

N NE E SE S SW W NW

TEMPERATURE

MAX./MIN. _____ °F / °C

PRECIPITATION

CONDITIONS

WIND

N NE E SE S SW W NW

TEMPERATURE

MAX./MIN. _____ °F / °C

PRECIPITATION

CONDITIONS

WIND

N NE E SE S SW W NW

And for the season it was winter, and they that know the winters of that country know them to be sharp and violent, and subject to cruel and fierce storms, dangerous to travel to known places, much more to search an unknown coast...

WILLIAM BRADFORD,
"OF PLYMOUTH PLANTATION"

MONDAY **1**	TUESDAY **2**	WEDNESDAY **3**

FRUIT

*When snow covers your paths
and your property,
observe the location
of the tracks you and
your family make around
the house and garden.
This may help you improve
path and garden design once
the snow has melted.*

FEBRUARY

M	T	W	T	F	S	S
1	2	3	4	5	6	7
8	9	10	11	12	13	14
15	16	17	18	19	20	21
22	23	24	25	26	27	28

TEMPERATURE

MAX./MIN. _____ °F /°C

PRECIPITATION

CONDITIONS

WIND

N NE E SE S SW W NW

TEMPERATURE

MAX./MIN. _____ °F /°C

PRECIPITATION

CONDITIONS

WIND

N NE E SE S SW W NW

TEMPERATURE

MAX./MIN. _____ °F /°C

PRECIPITATION

CONDITIONS

WIND

N NE E SE S SW W NW

THURSDAY 4

FRIDAY 5

SATURDAY 6

ROOT

1 2 3 4 5 6 7 8 9 10 11 12 1 2 3 4 5 6 7 8 9 10 11 12

TEMPERATURE

MAX./MIN. _____ °F / °C

PRECIPITATION

CONDITIONS

WIND

N NE E SE S SW W NW

SUNDAY 7

FLOWER

1 2 3 4 5 6 7 8 9 10 11 12 1 2 3 4 5 6 7 8 9 10 11 12

TEMPERATURE

MAX./MIN. _____ °F / °C

PRECIPITATION

CONDITIONS

WIND

N NE E SE S SW W NW

TEMPERATURE

MAX./MIN. _____ °F / °C

PRECIPITATION

CONDITIONS

WIND

N NE E SE S SW W NW

TEMPERATURE

MAX./MIN. _____ °F / °C

PRECIPITATION

CONDITIONS

WIND

N NE E SE S SW W NW

What is life?
It is the flash of a firefly
in the night.
It is the breath of a buffalo
in wintertime.
LAST WORDS OF CROWFOOT
(BLACKFOOT WARRIOR)

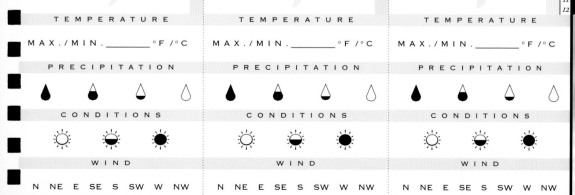

Build a birdfeeder
to attract birds,
one of nature's most efficient
predators of harmful bugs.
Replenish the birds'
water supply now and
keep it free of ice.

Contact local farms,
zoos, and stables to establish
a source of animal manure.

FEBRUARY

M	T	W	T	F	S	S
1	2	3	4	5	6	7
8	9	10	11	12	13	14
15	16	17	18	19	20	21
22	23	24	25	26	27	28

MONDAY 8

TUESDAY 9

WEDNESDAY 10

FLOWER

FLOWER

LEAF

LEAF

TEMPERATURE

MAX./MIN._____ °F /°C

PRECIPITATION

CONDITIONS

WIND

N NE E SE S SW W NW

TEMPERATURE

MAX./MIN._____ °F /°C

PRECIPITATION

CONDITIONS

WIND

N NE E SE S SW W NW

TEMPERATURE

MAX./MIN._____ °F /°C

PRECIPITATION

CONDITIONS

WIND

N NE E SE S SW W NW

THURSDAY 11

LEAF

FRUIT

TEMPERATURE

MAX./MIN. _____ °F /°C

PRECIPITATION

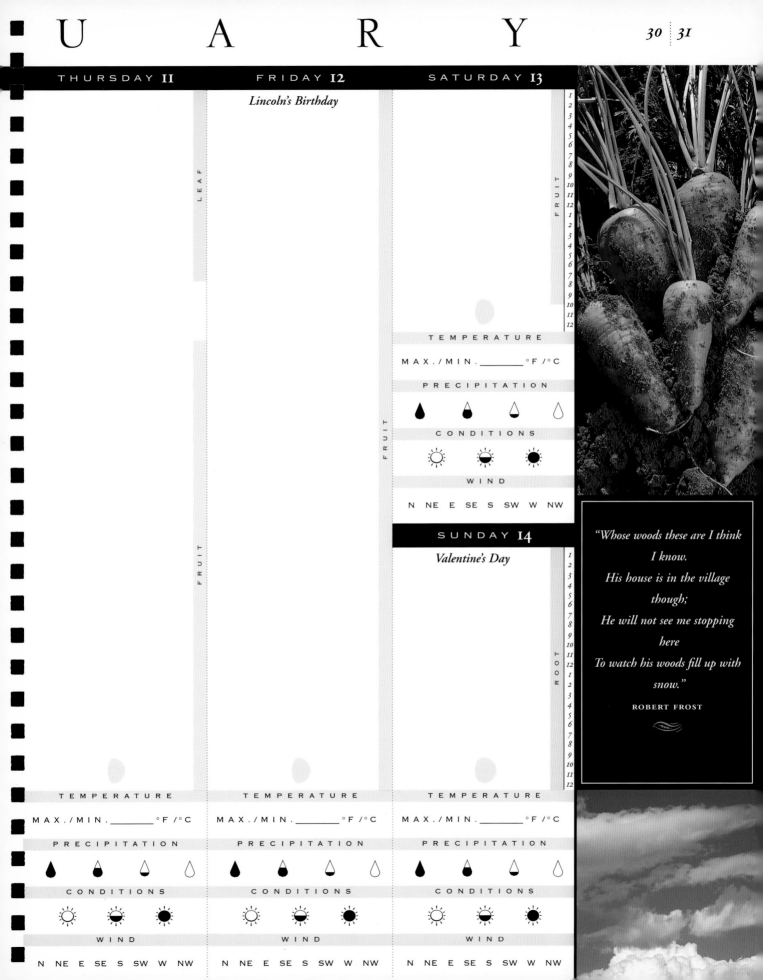

CONDITIONS

WIND

N NE E SE S SW W NW

FRIDAY 12

Lincoln's Birthday

TEMPERATURE

MAX./MIN. _____ °F /°C

PRECIPITATION

CONDITIONS

WIND

N NE E SE S SW W NW

SATURDAY 13

1 2 3 4 5 6 7 8 9 10 11 12
1 2 3 4 5 6 7 8 9 10 11 12

FRUIT

FRUIT

TEMPERATURE

MAX./MIN. _____ °F /°C

PRECIPITATION

CONDITIONS

WIND

N NE E SE S SW W NW

SUNDAY 14

Valentine's Day

1 2 3 4 5 6 7 8 9 10 11 12
1 2 3 4 5 6 7 8 9 10 11 12

ROOT

TEMPERATURE

MAX./MIN. _____ °F /°C

PRECIPITATION

CONDITIONS

WIND

N NE E SE S SW W NW

"Whose woods these are I think
I know.
His house is in the village
though;
He will not see me stopping
here
To watch his woods fill up with
snow."

ROBERT FROST

As the weather warms up,
root up perennial and
grassy weeds before
they have a chance to get
established
for the growing season.

Now is a good time
to check garden and
property fences and to repair
them if necessary.

FEBRUARY

M	T	W	T	F	S	S
1	2	3	4	5	6	7
8	9	10	11	12	13	14
15	16	17	18	19	20	21
22	23	24	25	26	27	28

MONDAY 15

*Washington's Birthday
(Observed)*

TUESDAY 16

Chinese New Year (4697)

ROOT

FLOWER

WEDNESDAY 17

Ash Wednesday

FLOWER

LEAF

TEMPERATURE

MAX./MIN. _____ °F /°C

PRECIPITATION

CONDITIONS

WIND

N NE E SE S SW W NW

TEMPERATURE

MAX./MIN. _____ °F /°C

PRECIPITATION

CONDITIONS

WIND

N NE E SE S SW W NW

TEMPERATURE

MAX./MIN. _____ °F /°C

PRECIPITATION

CONDITIONS

WIND

N NE E SE S SW W NW

THURSDAY 18

FRIDAY 19

SATURDAY 20

LEAF

1 2 3 4 5 6 7 8 9 10 11 12 1 2 3 4 5 6 7 8 9 10 11 12

LEAF

TEMPERATURE

MAX./MIN. _____ °F /°C

PRECIPITATION

CONDITIONS

WIND

N NE E SE S SW W NW

SUNDAY 21

FRUIT

1 2 3 4 5 6 7 8 9 10 11 12 1 2 3 4 5 6 7 8 9 10 11 12

All Nature seems at work.
Slugs leave their lair –
the Bees are stirring –
birds are on the wing –
And Winter slumbering in
the open air,
Wears on his face a dream
of Spring!

SAMUEL TAYLOR COLERIDGE,
"WORK WITHOUT HOPE"

TEMPERATURE

MAX./MIN. _____ °F /°C

PRECIPITATION

CONDITIONS

WIND

N NE E SE S SW W NW

TEMPERATURE

MAX./MIN. _____ °F /°C

PRECIPITATION

CONDITIONS

WIND

N NE E SE S SW W NW

TEMPERATURE

MAX./MIN. _____ °F /°C

PRECIPITATION

CONDITIONS

WIND

N NE E SE S SW W NW

| MONDAY **22** | TUESDAY **23** | WEDNESDAY **24** |

As the sun grows stronger, start pruning fruit trees; prune cleanly so the cuts heal easily.

Build (or prepare) your hotbeds and cold frames so seedlings can get a jump on spring.

FEBRUARY

M	T	W	T	F	S	S
1	2	3	4	5	6	7
8	9	10	11	12	13	14
15	16	17	18	19	20	21
22	23	24	25	26	27	28

ROOT

ROOT

ROOT

FLOWER

TEMPERATURE	TEMPERATURE	TEMPERATURE
MAX./MIN. _____ °F /°C	MAX./MIN. _____ °F /°C	MAX./MIN. _____ °F /°C
PRECIPITATION	PRECIPITATION	PRECIPITATION
CONDITIONS	CONDITIONS	CONDITIONS
WIND	WIND	WIND
N NE E SE S SW W NW	N NE E SE S SW W NW	N NE E SE S SW W NW

THURSDAY 25 | FRIDAY 26 | SATURDAY 27

LEAF

1 2 3 4 5 6 7 8 9 10 11 12

FLOWER

TEMPERATURE

MAX./MIN. _____ °F /°C

PRECIPITATION

CONDITIONS

WIND

N NE E SE S SW W NW

SUNDAY 28

LEAF

1 2 3 4 5 6 7 8 9 10 11 12

FLOWER

1 2 3 4 5 6 7 8 9 10 11 12

TEMPERATURE

MAX./MIN. _____ °F /°C

PRECIPITATION

CONDITIONS

WIND

N NE E SE S SW W NW

TEMPERATURE

MAX./MIN. _____ °F /°C

PRECIPITATION

CONDITIONS

WIND

N NE E SE S SW W NW

TEMPERATURE

MAX./MIN. _____ °F /°C

PRECIPITATION

CONDITIONS

WIND

N NE E SE S SW W NW

*The Night is mother
of the Day,
The Winter of the Spring,
And ever upon old Decay
The greenest mosses cling.*

JOHN GREENLEAF WHITTIER

*Let us give Nature a chance;
she knows her business
better than we do.*

MONTAIGNE

MONDAY 1

TUESDAY 2

WEDNESDAY 3

Prepare your seed and
plant labels.

Start your cabbage, onion,
broccoli, tomato, and
pepper seeds indoors now;
sit them on a windowsill and
let them enjoy
a sunny southern exposure.

MARCH

M	T	W	T	F	S	S
1	2	3	4	5	6	7
8	9	10	11	12	13	14
15	16	17	18	19	20	21
22	23	24	25	26	27	28
29	30	31				

FLOWER

LEAF

LEAF

FRUIT

ROOT

TEMPERATURE

MAX./MIN. _____ °F /°C

PRECIPITATION

CONDITIONS

WIND

N NE E SE S SW W NW

TEMPERATURE

MAX./MIN. _____ °F /°C

PRECIPITATION

CONDITIONS

WIND

N NE E SE S SW W NW

TEMPERATURE

MAX./MIN. _____ °F /°C

PRECIPITATION

CONDITIONS

WIND

N NE E SE S SW W NW

THURSDAY 4

FRIDAY 5

SATURDAY 6

ROOT

ROOT

ROOT

FLOWER

1
2
3
4
5
6
7
8
9
10
11
12
1
2
3
4
5
6
7
8
9
10
11
12

TEMPERATURE

MAX./MIN. _____ °F /°C

PRECIPITATION

CONDITIONS

WIND

N NE E SE S SW W NW

SUNDAY 7

FLOWER

1
2
3
4
5
6
7
8
9
10
11
12
1
2
3
4
5
6
7
8
9
10
11
12

Daffodils,
That come before the swallow
dares, and take
The Winds of March with
beauty

WILLIAM SHAKESPEARE

A Garden is a
lovesome thing.

THOMAS EDWARD BROWN

TEMPERATURE

MAX./MIN. _____ °F /°C

PRECIPITATION

CONDITIONS

WIND

N NE E SE S SW W NW

TEMPERATURE

MAX./MIN. _____ °F /°C

PRECIPITATION

CONDITIONS

WIND

N NE E SE S SW W NW

TEMPERATURE

MAX./MIN. _____ °F /°C

PRECIPITATION

CONDITIONS

WIND

N NE E SE S SW W NW

MONDAY 8

TUESDAY 9

WEDNESDAY 10

Plan to sow nitrogen-rich green manure cover crops such as vetch, clover, and fava beans and dig them under before they flower.

Read a book about composting.

MARCH

M	T	W	T	F	S	S
1	2	3	4	5	6	7
8	9	10	11	12	13	14
15	16	17	18	19	20	21
22	23	24	25	26	27	28
29	30	31				

FLOWER

LEAF

LEAF

LEAF

FRUIT

TEMPERATURE

MAX./MIN. _____ °F /°C

PRECIPITATION

CONDITIONS

WIND

N NE E SE S SW W NW

TEMPERATURE

MAX./MIN. _____ °F /°C

PRECIPITATION

CONDITIONS

WIND

N NE E SE S SW W NW

TEMPERATURE

MAX./MIN. _____ °F /°C

PRECIPITATION

CONDITIONS

WIND

N NE E SE S SW W NW

THURSDAY 11   **FRIDAY 12**   **SATURDAY 13**

FRUIT

1 2 3 4 5 6 7 8 9 10 11 12

ROOT

1 2 3 4 5 6 7 8 9 10 11 12

FRUIT

TEMPERATURE

MAX./MIN. _____ °F /°C

PRECIPITATION

CONDITIONS

WIND

N NE E SE S SW W NW

SUNDAY 14

ROOT

1 2 3 4 5 6 7 8 9 10 11 12 1 2 3 4 5 6 7 8 9 10 11 12

There is no good arguing
with the inevitable.
The only argument available
with an east wind
is to put on your overcoat.

JAMES RUSSELL LOWELL

Holy Mother Earth,
the trees and all nature
are witnesses
of your thoughts and deeds.

WINNEBAGO SAYING

TEMPERATURE

MAX./MIN. _____ °F /°C

PRECIPITATION

CONDITIONS

WIND

N NE E SE S SW W NW

TEMPERATURE

MAX./MIN. _____ °F /°C

PRECIPITATION

CONDITIONS

WIND

N NE E SE S SW W NW

TEMPERATURE

MAX./MIN. _____ °F /°C

PRECIPITATION

CONDITIONS

WIND

N NE E SE S SW W NW

MONDAY **15**	TUESDAY **16**	WEDNESDAY **17**
		St. Patrick's Day

*Organize your seed packets
by planting date
so they are ready and
in sequence come
planting time.*

*Warm the soil with
pegged sheets of clear plastic,
especially in cooler regions;
to control weeds,
cover the clear plastic
with black plastic.*

ROOT

FLOWER

FLOWER

LEAF

MARCH

M	T	W	T	F	S	S
1	2	3	4	5	6	7
8	9	10	11	12	13	14
15	16	17	18	19	20	21
22	23	24	25	26	27	28
29	30	31				

TEMPERATURE

MAX./MIN. _____ °F /°C

PRECIPITATION

CONDITIONS

WIND

N NE E SE S SW W NW

TEMPERATURE

MAX./MIN. _____ °F /°C

PRECIPITATION

CONDITIONS

WIND

N NE E SE S SW W NW

TEMPERATURE

MAX./MIN. _____ °F /°C

PRECIPITATION

CONDITIONS

WIND

N NE E SE S SW W NW

THURSDAY 18

FRIDAY 19

SATURDAY 20

LEAF

FRUIT

1
2
3
4
5
6
7
8
9
10
11
12
1
2
3
4
5
6
7
8
9
10
11
12

TEMPERATURE

MAX./MIN. _____°F /°C

PRECIPITATION

CONDITIONS

WIND

N NE E SE S SW W NW

SUNDAY 21

Spring Begins

FRUIT

ROOT

1
2
3
4
5
6
7
8
9
10
11
12
1
2
3
4
5
6
7
8
9
10
11
12

LEAF

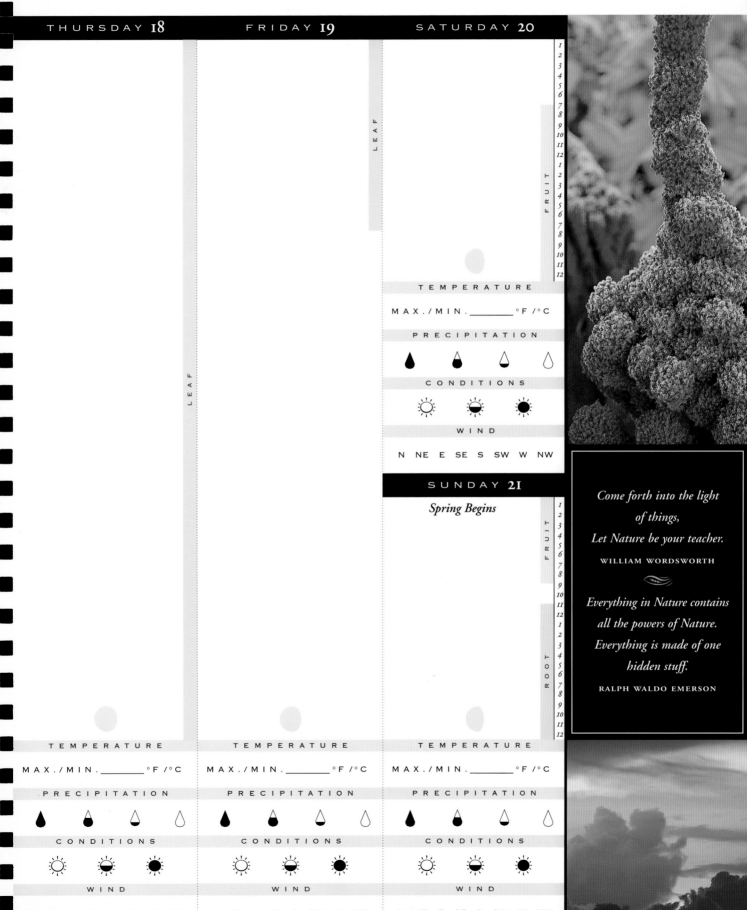

*Come forth into the light
of things,
Let Nature be your teacher.*
WILLIAM WORDSWORTH

*Everything in Nature contains
all the powers of Nature.
Everything is made of one
hidden stuff.*
RALPH WALDO EMERSON

TEMPERATURE

MAX./MIN. _____°F /°C

PRECIPITATION

CONDITIONS

WIND

N NE E SE S SW W NW

TEMPERATURE

MAX./MIN. _____°F /°C

PRECIPITATION

CONDITIONS

WIND

N NE E SE S SW W NW

TEMPERATURE

MAX./MIN. _____°F /°C

PRECIPITATION

CONDITIONS

WIND

N NE E SE S SW W NW

For winter's rains and
ruins are over,
And all the season of
snow and sins;
The days dividing
lover and lover,
The light that loses,
the night that wins;
And time remembered
is grief forgotten,
And frosts are slain
and flowers begotten,
And in green underwood
and cover
Blossom by blossom
the spring begins.

ALGERNON CHARLES SWINBURNE

> *Buy starts early
> in the season when selection
> is at its best.*
>
> *Begin digging your soil and
> applying cured fall
> compost and organic
> fertilizer.*

MARCH

M	T	W	T	F	S	S
1	2	3	4	5	6	7
8	9	10	11	12	13	14
15	16	17	18	19	20	21
22	23	24	25	26	27	28
29	30	31				

MONDAY 22	TUESDAY 23	WEDNESDAY 24

1 2 3 4 5 6 7 8 9 10 11 12 1 2 3 4 5 6 7 8 9 10 11 12

ROOT

ROOT

FLOWER

MONDAY 22

TEMPERATURE

MAX./MIN. _____ °F /°C

PRECIPITATION

CONDITIONS

WIND

N NE E SE S SW W NW

TUESDAY 23

TEMPERATURE

MAX./MIN. _____ °F /°C

PRECIPITATION

CONDITIONS

WIND

N NE E SE S SW W NW

WEDNESDAY 24

TEMPERATURE

MAX./MIN. _____ °F /°C

PRECIPITATION

CONDITIONS

WIND

N NE E SE S SW W NW

THURSDAY 25

FRIDAY 26

SATURDAY 27

LEAF

1 2 3 4 5 6 7 8 9 10 11 12 1 2 3 4 5 6 7 8 9 10 11 12

TEMPERATURE

MAX./MIN. _____ °F /°C

PRECIPITATION

CONDITIONS

WIND

N NE E SE S SW W NW

FLOWER

LEAF

SUNDAY 28

Palm Sunday

FRUIT

1 2 3 4 5 6 7 8 9 10 11 12 1 2 3 4 5 6 7 8 9 10 11 12

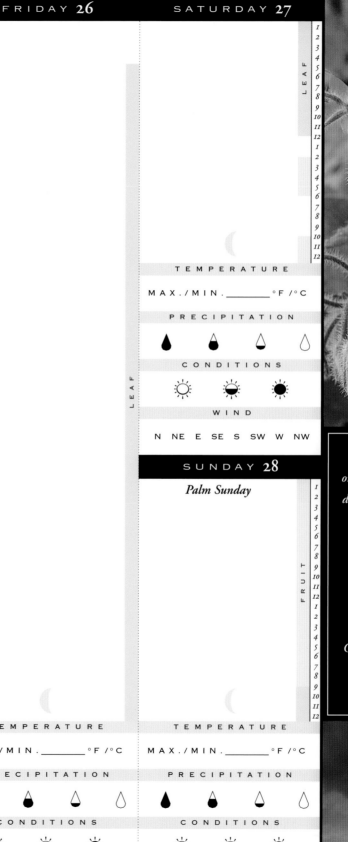

The first day of spring is
one thing, and the first spring
day is another. The difference
between them is sometimes
as great as a month.

HENRY VAN DYKE,
"FISHERMAN'S LUCK"
(1899)

Come, gently spring! ethereal
mildness, come.

JAMES THOMSON

TEMPERATURE

MAX./MIN. _____ °F /°C

PRECIPITATION

CONDITIONS

WIND

N NE E SE S SW W NW

TEMPERATURE

MAX./MIN. _____ °F /°C

PRECIPITATION

CONDITIONS

WIND

N NE E SE S SW W NW

TEMPERATURE

MAX./MIN. _____ °F /°C

PRECIPITATION

CONDITIONS

WIND

N NE E SE S SW W NW

MONDAY 29	TUESDAY 30	WEDNESDAY 31

I
2
3
4
5
6
7
8
9
I0
II
I2
I
2
3
4
5
6
7
8
9
I0
II
I2

LEAF
FRUIT
FRUIT
ROOT
LEAF
LEAF
ROOT

Start a new compost pile now. Dig the ground on which it will stand to a depth of one foot, to help aeration and drainage.

Mulch plants to discourage weeds and to protect the surrounding soil from the elements.

APRIL

M	T	W	T	F	S	S
			I	2	3	4
5	6	7	8	9	I0	II
I2	I3	I4	I5	I6	I7	I8
I9	20	2I	22	23	24	25
26	27	28	29	30		

TEMPERATURE

MAX./MIN. _____ °F /°C

PRECIPITATION

CONDITIONS

WIND

N NE E SE S SW W NW

TEMPERATURE

MAX./MIN. _____ °F /°C

PRECIPITATION

CONDITIONS

WIND

N NE E SE S SW W NW

TEMPERATURE

MAX./MIN. _____ °F /°C

PRECIPITATION

CONDITIONS

WIND

N NE E SE S SW W NW

THURSDAY 1

Passover

FRIDAY 2

Good Friday

ROOT

SATURDAY 3

1 2 3 4 5 6 7 8 9 10 11 12 1 2 3 4 5 6 7 8 9 10 11 12

ROOT

TEMPERATURE

MAX./MIN. _____ °F /°C

PRECIPITATION

CONDITIONS

WIND

N NE E SE S SW W NW

SUNDAY 4

**Easter Sunday
Daylight Saving Time begins**

FLOWER

1 2 3 4 5 6 7 8 9 10 11 12 1 2 3 4 5 6 7 8 9 10 11 12

TEMPERATURE

MAX./MIN. _____ °F /°C

PRECIPITATION

CONDITIONS

WIND

N NE E SE S SW W NW

TEMPERATURE

MAX./MIN. _____ °F /°C

PRECIPITATION

CONDITIONS

WIND

N NE E SE S SW W NW

TEMPERATURE

MAX./MIN. _____ °F /°C

PRECIPITATION

CONDITIONS

WIND

N NE E SE S SW W NW

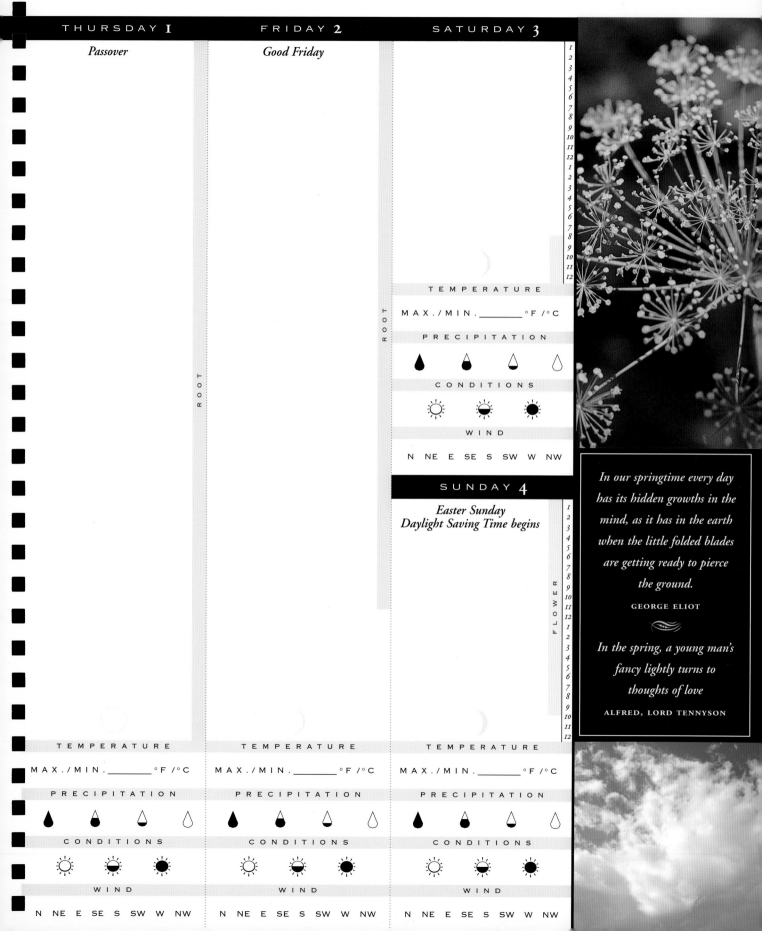

*In our springtime every day
has its hidden growths in the
mind, as it has in the earth
when the little folded blades
are getting ready to pierce
the ground.*

GEORGE ELIOT

*In the spring, a young man's
fancy lightly turns to
thoughts of love*

ALFRED, LORD TENNYSON

MONDAY 5	TUESDAY 6	WEDNESDAY 7

1
2
3
4
5
6
7
8
9
10
11
12
1
2
3
4
5
6
7
8
9
10
11
12

Prepare your planting beds.

Plant African marigolds now and turn them under in June before transplanting tomatoes. The marigolds will protect the tomatoes from fungal wilt.

Transplant your starts.

LEAF

LEAF

FRUIT

APRIL

M	T	W	T	F	S	S
			1	2	3	4
5	6	7	8	9	10	11
12	13	14	15	16	17	18
19	20	21	22	23	24	25
26	27	28	29	30		

TEMPERATURE
MAX./MIN. _____ °F /°C
PRECIPITATION
CONDITIONS
WIND
N NE E SE S SW W NW

TEMPERATURE
MAX./MIN. _____ °F /°C
PRECIPITATION
CONDITIONS
WIND
N NE E SE S SW W NW

TEMPERATURE
MAX./MIN. _____ °F /°C
PRECIPITATION
CONDITIONS
WIND
N NE E SE S SW W NW

THURSDAY 8

FRIDAY 9

SATURDAY 10

FRUIT

ROOT

1
2
3
4
5
6
7
8
9
10
11
12
1
2
3
4
5
6
7
8
9
10
11
12

FRUIT

TEMPERATURE

MAX./MIN. _____ °F /°C

PRECIPITATION

CONDITIONS

WIND

N NE E SE S SW W NW

SUNDAY 11

ROOT

1
2
3
4
5
6
7
8
9
10
11
12
1
2
3
4
5
6
7
8
9
10
11
12

ROOT

ROOT

> It's a warm wind, the west
> wind, full of birds' cries;
> I never hear the west wind
> but tears are in my eyes.
> For it comes from the west
> lands, the old brown hills,
> And April's in the west wind,
> and daffodils.
>
> JOHN MASEFIELD

TEMPERATURE

MAX./MIN. _____ °F /°C

PRECIPITATION

CONDITIONS

WIND

N NE E SE S SW W NW

TEMPERATURE

MAX./MIN. _____ °F /°C

PRECIPITATION

CONDITIONS

WIND

N NE E SE S SW W NW

TEMPERATURE

MAX./MIN. _____ °F /°C

PRECIPITATION

CONDITIONS

WIND

N NE E SE S SW W NW

MONDAY 12 **TUESDAY 13** **WEDNESDAY 14**

*The Earth returns to kindness;
the sounds long muffled
by winter are released.
Feel the strength
of the sun growing.*

*Release ladybugs
in the early spring
so they can feed on aphids
and other harmful insects.
Avoid releasing them
in sunshine.*

FLOWER

LEAF

APRIL

M	T	W	T	F	S	S
			1	2	3	4
5	6	7	8	9	10	11
12	13	14	15	16	17	18
19	20	21	22	23	24	25
26	27	28	29	30		

TEMPERATURE MAX./MIN. _____ °F /°C
PRECIPITATION
CONDITIONS
WIND N NE E SE S SW W NW

TEMPERATURE MAX./MIN. _____ °F /°C
PRECIPITATION
CONDITIONS
WIND N NE E SE S SW W NW

TEMPERATURE MAX./MIN. _____ °F /°C
PRECIPITATION
CONDITIONS
WIND N NE E SE S SW W NW

THURSDAY **15**

FRIDAY **16**

SATURDAY **17**

Muslim New Year

ROOT

1
2
3
4
5
6
7
8
9
10
11
12
1
2
3
4
5
6
7
8
9
10
11
12

LEAF

FRUIT

TEMPERATURE

MAX./MIN. _____ °F /°C

PRECIPITATION

CONDITIONS

WIND

N NE E SE S SW W NW

SUNDAY **18**

ROOT

1
2
3
4
5
6
7
8
9
10
11
12
1
2
3
4
5
6
7
8
9
10
11
12

ROOT

April is the cruellest month,
breeding
Lilacs out of the dead land,
mixing
Memory and desire, stirring
Dull roots with spring rain

T. S. ELIOT

TEMPERATURE

MAX./MIN. _____ °F /°C

PRECIPITATION

CONDITIONS

WIND

N NE E SE S SW W NW

TEMPERATURE

MAX./MIN. _____ °F /°C

PRECIPITATION

CONDITIONS

WIND

N NE E SE S SW W NW

TEMPERATURE

MAX./MIN. _____ °F /°C

PRECIPITATION

CONDITIONS

WIND

N NE E SE S SW W NW

MONDAY **19**	TUESDAY **20**	WEDNESDAY **21**

*Try using powdered ginger
around plants
to keep slugs and snails at bay;
or use thin copper sheeting
half buried in the ground.*

*Prune your perennial herbs
(except for sage) to encourage
thick, bushier growth.*

APRIL

M	T	W	T	F	S	S
			1	2	3	4
5	6	7	8	9	10	11
12	13	14	15	16	17	18
19	20	21	22	23	24	25
26	27	28	29	30		

ROOT

ROOT

FLOWER

FLOWER

FLOWER

TEMPERATURE	TEMPERATURE	TEMPERATURE
MAX./MIN. _____ °F /°C	MAX./MIN. _____ °F /°C	MAX./MIN. _____ °F /°C
PRECIPITATION	PRECIPITATION	PRECIPITATION
CONDITIONS	CONDITIONS	CONDITIONS
WIND	WIND	WIND
N NE E SE S SW W NW	N NE E SE S SW W NW	N NE E SE S SW W NW

THURSDAY 22   FRIDAY 23   SATURDAY 24

FLOWER

FRUIT

1
2
3
4
5
6
7
8
9
10
11
12
1
2
3
4
5
6
7
8
9
10
11
12

LEAF

TEMPERATURE

MAX./MIN. _____ °F / °C

PRECIPITATION

CONDITIONS

WIND

N NE E SE S SW W NW

LEAF

SUNDAY 25

FRUIT

1
2
3
4
5
6
7
8
9
10
11
12
1
2
3
4
5
6
7
8
9
10
11
12

LEAF

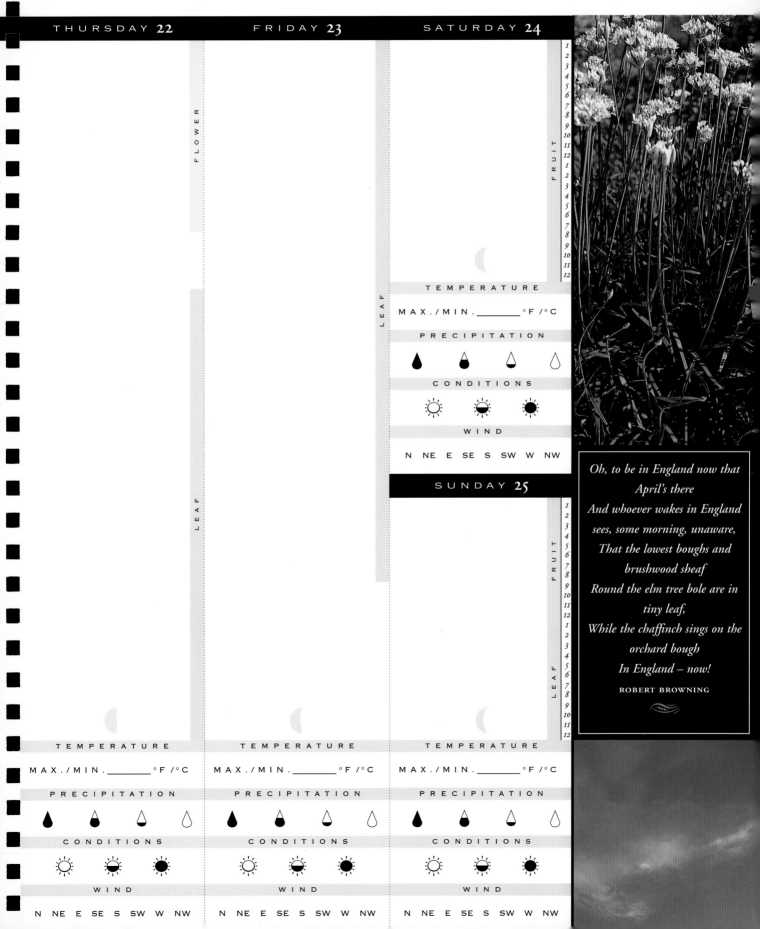

*Oh, to be in England now that
April's there
And whoever wakes in England
sees, some morning, unaware,
That the lowest boughs and
brushwood sheaf
Round the elm tree bole are in
tiny leaf,
While the chaffinch sings on the
orchard bough
In England – now!*

ROBERT BROWNING

TEMPERATURE

MAX./MIN._____ °F / °C

PRECIPITATION

CONDITIONS

WIND

N NE E SE S SW W NW

TEMPERATURE

MAX./MIN._____ °F / °C

PRECIPITATION

CONDITIONS

WIND

N NE E SE S SW W NW

TEMPERATURE

MAX./MIN._____ °F / °C

PRECIPITATION

CONDITIONS

WIND

N NE E SE S SW W NW

MONDAY 26   **TUESDAY 27**   **WEDNESDAY 28**

It is the time to plant!

*Plant beneficial insect refuges
to provide habitat.*

*The many shades of green
fill the landscape.*

APRIL

M	T	W	T	F	S	S
			1	2	3	4
5	6	7	8	9	10	11
12	13	14	15	16	17	18
19	20	21	22	23	24	25
26	27	28	29	30		

ROOT   ROOT   ROOT

TEMPERATURE

MAX./MIN. _____ °F /°C

PRECIPITATION

CONDITIONS

WIND

N NE E SE S SW W NW

TEMPERATURE

MAX./MIN. _____ °F /°C

PRECIPITATION

CONDITIONS

WIND

N NE E SE S SW W NW

TEMPERATURE

MAX./MIN. _____ °F /°C

PRECIPITATION

CONDITIONS

WIND

N NE E SE S SW W NW

THURSDAY **29**	FRIDAY **30**	SATURDAY **1**
	Arbor Day	*May Day*

ROOT

ROOT

FLOWER

1 2 3 4 5 6 7 8 9 10 11 12 1 2 3 4 5 6 7 8 9 10 11 12

TEMPERATURE

MAX./MIN. _____ °F /°C

PRECIPITATION

CONDITIONS

WIND

N NE E SE S SW W NW

FLOWER

SUNDAY **2**

1 2 3 4 5 6 7 8 9 10 11 12 1 2 3 4 5 6 7 8 9 10 11 12

LEAF

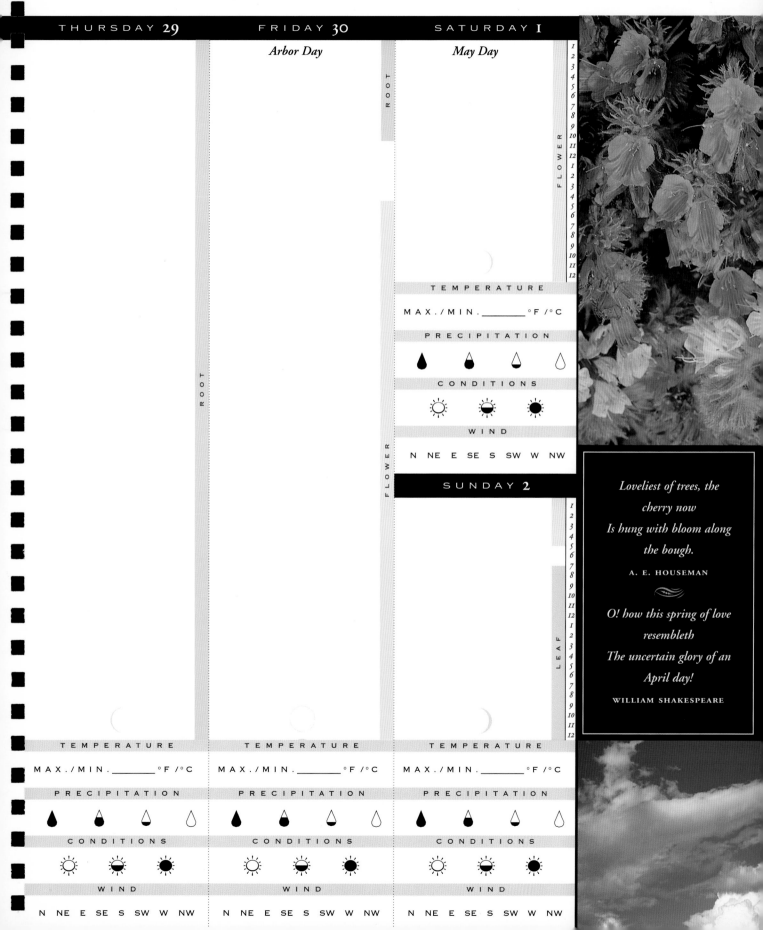

> Loveliest of trees, the
> cherry now
> Is hung with bloom along
> the bough.
>
> **A. E. HOUSEMAN**
>
> *O! how this spring of love
> resembleth
> The uncertain glory of an
> April day!*
>
> **WILLIAM SHAKESPEARE**

TEMPERATURE

MAX./MIN. _____ °F /°C

PRECIPITATION

CONDITIONS

WIND

N NE E SE S SW W NW

TEMPERATURE

MAX./MIN. _____ °F /°C

PRECIPITATION

CONDITIONS

WIND

N NE E SE S SW W NW

TEMPERATURE

MAX./MIN. _____ °F /°C

PRECIPITATION

CONDITIONS

WIND

N NE E SE S SW W NW

MONDAY 3

TUESDAY 4

WEDNESDAY 5

Cinco de Mayo

LEAF

LEAF

FRUIT

FRUIT

*In general, plant seeds
two to three times
their thickness in the soil.
Cover them and keep them
moist but not flooded.*

*Be vigilant!
Late frosts often occur
during the last week before
a full moon, if the sky is clear
and the air is calm.*

MAY

M	T	W	T	F	S	S
					1	2
3	4	5	6	7	8	9
10	11	12	13	14	15	16
17	18	19	20	21	22	23
24/31	25	26	27	28	29	30

1 2 3 4 5 6 7 8 9 10 11 12 1 2 3 4 5 6 7 8 9 10 11 12

TEMPERATURE

MAX./MIN. _____ °F /°C

PRECIPITATION

CONDITIONS

WIND

N NE E SE S SW W NW

TEMPERATURE

MAX./MIN. _____ °F /°C

PRECIPITATION

CONDITIONS

WIND

N NE E SE S SW W NW

TEMPERATURE

MAX./MIN. _____ °F /°C

PRECIPITATION

CONDITIONS

WIND

N NE E SE S SW W NW

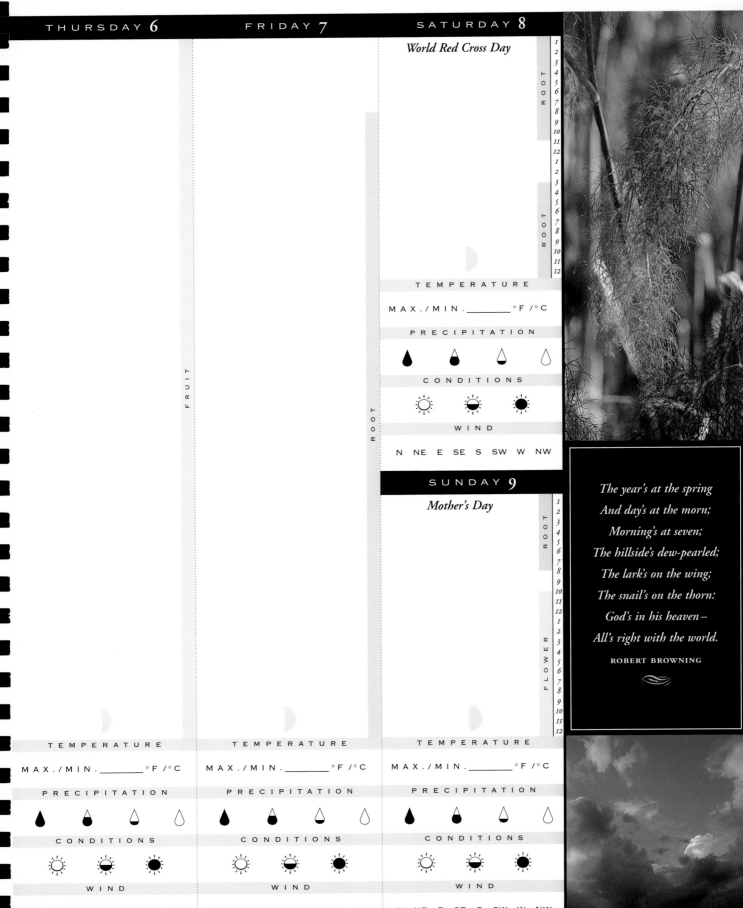

THURSDAY 6

FRIDAY 7

FRUIT

SATURDAY 8

World Red Cross Day

ROOT

1 2 3 4 5 6 7 8 9 10 11 12

ROOT

1 2 3 4 5 6 7 8 9 10 11 12

ROOT

TEMPERATURE

MAX./MIN. _____ °F /°C

PRECIPITATION

CONDITIONS

WIND

N NE E SE S SW W NW

SUNDAY 9

Mother's Day

ROOT

1 2 3 4 5 6 7 8 9 10 11 12

FLOWER

1 2 3 4 5 6 7 8 9 10 11 12

The year's at the spring
And day's at the morn;
Morning's at seven;
The hillside's dew-pearled;
The lark's on the wing;
The snail's on the thorn:
God's in his heaven –
All's right with the world.

ROBERT BROWNING

TEMPERATURE

MAX./MIN. _____ °F /°C

PRECIPITATION

CONDITIONS

WIND

N NE E SE S SW W NW

TEMPERATURE

MAX./MIN. _____ °F /°C

PRECIPITATION

CONDITIONS

WIND

N NE E SE S SW W NW

TEMPERATURE

MAX./MIN. _____ °F /°C

PRECIPITATION

CONDITIONS

WIND

N NE E SE S SW W NW

MONDAY 10 **TUESDAY 11** **WEDNESDAY 12**

FLOWER

LEAF

LEAF

Shadows run longer every day.

*Stagger your planting
of crops such as
tomatoes, lettuces, radishes,
and green beans
at intervals of ten days to
two weeks to ensure a longer,
steady harvest.*

*Begin placing insect traps
in fruit trees.*

MAY

M	T	W	T	F	S	S
					1	*2*
3	*4*	*5*	*6*	*7*	*8*	*9*
10	*11*	*12*	*13*	*14*	*15*	*16*
17	*18*	*19*	*20*	*21*	*22*	*23*
24/31	*25*	*26*	*27*	*28*	*29*	*30*

TEMPERATURE
MAX./MIN. _____ °F /°C
PRECIPITATION
CONDITIONS
WIND
N NE E SE S SW W NW

TEMPERATURE
MAX./MIN. _____ °F /°C
PRECIPITATION
CONDITIONS
WIND
N NE E SE S SW W NW

TEMPERATURE
MAX./MIN. _____ °F /°C
PRECIPITATION
CONDITIONS
WIND
N NE E SE S SW W NW

THURSDAY 13

FRIDAY 14

SATURDAY 15

1
2
3
4
5
6
7
8
9
10
11
12
1
2
3
4
5
6
7
8
9
10
11
12

L E A F

F R U I T

TEMPERATURE

MAX./MIN. _____ °F / °C

PRECIPITATION

CONDITIONS

WIND

N   NE   E   SE   S   SW   W   NW

SUNDAY 16

R O O T

1
2
3
4
5
6
7
8
9
10
11
12
1
2
3
4
5
6
7
8
9
10
11
12

*Spring, the sweet spring, is
the year's pleasant king;
Then blooms each thing, then
maids dance in a ring,
Cold doth not sting, the pretty
birds do sing.
Cuckoo, jug-jug, pu-we,
to-witta-woo!*

THOMAS NASHE

TEMPERATURE

MAX./MIN. _____ °F / °C

PRECIPITATION

CONDITIONS

WIND

N   NE   E   SE   S   SW   W   NW

TEMPERATURE

MAX./MIN. _____ °F / °C

PRECIPITATION

CONDITIONS

WIND

N   NE   E   SE   S   SW   W   NW

TEMPERATURE

MAX./MIN. _____ °F / °C

PRECIPITATION

CONDITIONS

WIND

N   NE   E   SE   S   SW   W   NW

MONDAY **17**	TUESDAY **18**	WEDNESDAY **19**

*Release beneficial insects
to establish colonies
for the growing season.*

*Invite a local beekeeper
to place a hive or two
in your orchard or garden.
Even better, do your homework
and plan to keep bees
yourself.*

MAY

M	T	W	T	F	S	S
					I	2
3	4	5	6	7	8	9
10	11	12	13	14	15	16
17	18	19	20	21	22	23
24/31	25	26	27	28	29	30

ROOT

FLOWER

FLOWER

FLOWER

LEAF

TEMPERATURE

MAX./MIN. _____ °F /°C

PRECIPITATION

CONDITIONS

WIND

N NE E SE S SW W NW

TEMPERATURE

MAX./MIN. _____ °F /°C

PRECIPITATION

CONDITIONS

WIND

N NE E SE S SW W NW

TEMPERATURE

MAX./MIN. _____ °F /°C

PRECIPITATION

CONDITIONS

WIND

N NE E SE S SW W NW

THURSDAY 20

FRIDAY 21

SATURDAY 22

LEAF

FRUIT

1 2 3 4 5 6 7 8 9 10 11 12 1 2 3 4 5 6 7 8 9 10 11 12

TEMPERATURE

MAX./MIN. _____ °F /°C

PRECIPITATION

CONDITIONS

WIND

N NE E SE S SW W NW

SUNDAY 23

FRUIT

1 2 3 4 5 6 7 8 9 10 11 12 1 2 3 4 5 6 7 8 9 10 11 12

TEMPERATURE

MAX./MIN. _____ °F /°C

PRECIPITATION

CONDITIONS

WIND

N NE E SE S SW W NW

TEMPERATURE

MAX./MIN. _____ °F /°C

PRECIPITATION

CONDITIONS

WIND

N NE E SE S SW W NW

TEMPERATURE

MAX./MIN. _____ °F /°C

PRECIPITATION

CONDITIONS

WIND

N NE E SE S SW W NW

*The month of May was come,
when every lusty heart
beginneth to blossom,
and to bring forth fruit;
for, like as herbs and trees bring
forth fruit and flourish in May,
in likewise every lusty heart
that is in any manner a lover,
springeth and flourisheth
in lusty deeds. For it giveth
unto all lovers courage,
that lusty month of May.*

SIR THOMAS MALORY

MONDAY 24   **TUESDAY 25**   **WEDNESDAY 26**

Victoria Day (Canada)

ROOT

ROOT

ROOT

The strawberry harvest begins.

*Keep your compost layered,
like lasagna!
A two-inch layer of brown
(dry) vegetation, then an equal
amount of green vegetation
or household waste,
and then an equal layer of soil.
Using only kitchen waste
works too; the compost will just
take longer to "cure."*

MAY

M	T	W	T	F	S	S
				1	2	
				1	*2*	
3	*4*	*5*	*6*	*7*	*8*	*9*
10	*11*	*12*	*13*	*14*	*15*	*16*
17	*18*	*19*	*20*	*21*	*22*	*23*
24/31	*25*	*26*	*27*	*28*	*29*	*30*

TEMPERATURE
MAX./MIN. _____ °F /°C
PRECIPITATION
CONDITIONS
WIND
N NE E SE S SW W NW

TEMPERATURE
MAX./MIN. _____ °F /°C
PRECIPITATION
CONDITIONS
WIND
N NE E SE S SW W NW

TEMPERATURE
MAX./MIN. _____ °F /°C
PRECIPITATION
CONDITIONS
WIND
N NE E SE S SW W NW

THURSDAY 27	FRIDAY 28	SATURDAY 29

ROOT

FLOWER

LEAF

FLOWER

SATURDAY 29

TEMPERATURE

MAX./MIN. _____ °F /°C

PRECIPITATION

CONDITIONS

WIND

N NE E SE S SW W NW

SUNDAY 30

LEAF

*Shall I compare thee to a
summer's day?
Thou art more lovely and
more temperate:
Rough winds do shake the
darling buds of May,
And summer's lease hath
all too short a date.*

WILLIAM SHAKESPEARE

THURSDAY 27

TEMPERATURE

MAX./MIN. _____ °F /°C

PRECIPITATION

CONDITIONS

WIND

N NE E SE S SW W NW

FRIDAY 28

TEMPERATURE

MAX./MIN. _____ °F /°C

PRECIPITATION

CONDITIONS

WIND

N NE E SE S SW W NW

SUNDAY 30

TEMPERATURE

MAX./MIN. _____ °F /°C

PRECIPITATION

CONDITIONS

WIND

N NE E SE S SW W NW

| MONDAY **31** | TUESDAY **I** | WEDNESDAY **2** |

Memorial Day (Observed)

ROOT

FRUIT

FRUIT

FRUIT

I
2
3
4
5
6
7
8
9
10
II
12
I
2
3
4
5
6
7
8
9
10
II
12

*Once your corn plants have
begun growing, sow
a nitrogen-fixing cover crop
such as clover between
the corn plants to maximize
nutrients and minimize weeds.*

*Prepare pole-and-string
trellises for training your
climbing beans;
yields will more than
justify the effort.*

JUNE

M	T	W	T	F	S	S
	I	*2*	*3*	*4*	*5*	*6*
7	*8*	*9*	*10*	*II*	*12*	*13*
14	*15*	*16*	*17*	*18*	*19*	*20*
21	*22*	*23*	*24*	*25*	*26*	*27*
28	*29*	*30*				

T E M P E R A T U R E

MAX./MIN. _____ °F /°C

P R E C I P I T A T I O N

C O N D I T I O N S

W I N D

N NE E SE S SW W NW

T E M P E R A T U R E

MAX./MIN. _____ °F /°C

P R E C I P I T A T I O N

C O N D I T I O N S

W I N D

N NE E SE S SW W NW

T E M P E R A T U R E

MAX./MIN. _____ °F /°C

P R E C I P I T A T I O N

C O N D I T I O N S

W I N D

N NE E SE S SW W NW

THURSDAY 3

FRUIT

ROOT

FRIDAY 4

ROOT

SATURDAY 5

ROOT

FLOWER

1 2 3 4 5 6 7 8 9 10 11 12 1 2 3 4 5 6 7 8 9 10 11 12

TEMPERATURE

MAX./MIN. _____ °F /°C

PRECIPITATION

CONDITIONS

WIND

N NE E SE S SW W NW

SUNDAY 6

ROOT

FLOWER

1 2 3 4 5 6 7 8 9 10 11 12 1 2 3 4 5 6 7 8 9 10 11 12

*Now 'tis the spring, and weeds
are shallow-rooted;
Suffer them now and they'll
o'ergrow the garden.*

WILLIAM SHAKESPEARE

June is bustin' out all over.

OSCAR HAMMERSTEIN II

TEMPERATURE

MAX./MIN. _____ °F /°C

PRECIPITATION

CONDITIONS

WIND

N NE E SE S SW W NW

TEMPERATURE

MAX./MIN. _____ °F /°C

PRECIPITATION

CONDITIONS

WIND

N NE E SE S SW W NW

TEMPERATURE

MAX./MIN. _____ °F /°C

PRECIPITATION

CONDITIONS

WIND

N NE E SE S SW W NW

J   U

*Use netting to keep birds away
from your soft fruit.
Best to construct a cage
rather than risk breaking twigs
by draping the netting.
Bury the bottom
of the netting in the ground.*

*Observe your plants continually
and keep weeds in check.*

FLOWER

LEAF

LEAF

LEAF

JUNE

M	T	W	T	F	S	S
	1	2	3	4	5	6
7	8	9	10	11	12	13
14	15	16	17	18	19	20
21	22	23	24	25	26	27
28	29	30				

1
2
3
4
5
6
7
8
9
10
11
12
1
2
3
4
5
6
7
8
9
10
11
12

TEMPERATURE

MAX./MIN. _____ °F /°C

PRECIPITATION

CONDITIONS

WIND

N NE E SE S SW W NW

TEMPERATURE

MAX./MIN. _____ °F /°C

PRECIPITATION

CONDITIONS

WIND

N NE E SE S SW W NW

TEMPERATURE

MAX./MIN. _____ °F /°C

PRECIPITATION

CONDITIONS

WIND

N NE E SE S SW W NW

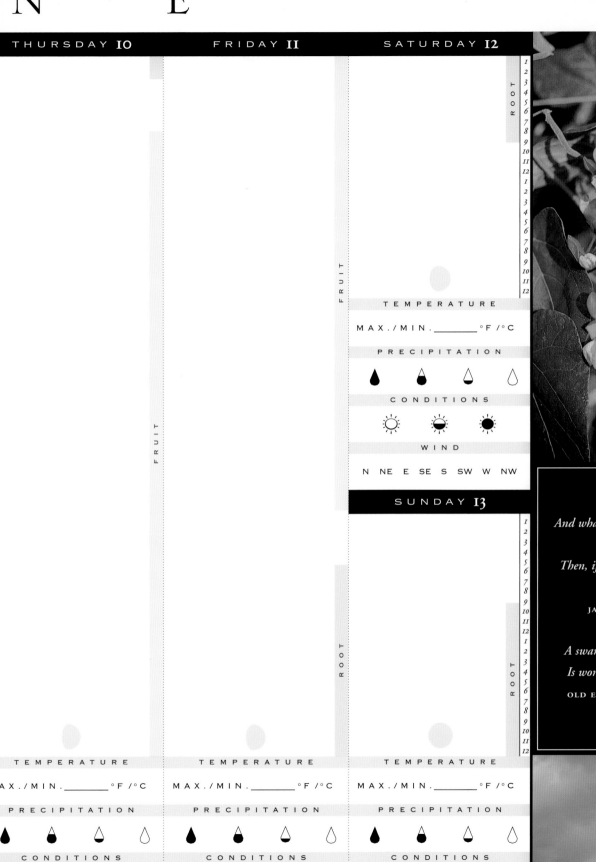

THURSDAY 10

FRIDAY 11

SATURDAY 12

ROOT

I 2 3 4 5 6 7 8 9 10 11 12 I 2 3 4 5 6 7 8 9 11 12

FRUIT

FRUIT

TEMPERATURE

MAX. / MIN. _____ °F / °C

PRECIPITATION

CONDITIONS

WIND

N NE E SE S SW W NW

SUNDAY 13

ROOT

I 2 3 4 5 6 7 8 9 10 11 12 I 2 3 4 5 6 7 8 9 10 11 12

ROOT

And what is so rare as a day
in June?
Then, if ever, come perfect
days.

JAMES LOWELL

A swarm of bees in June
Is worth a silver spoon.

OLD ENGLISH PROVERB

TEMPERATURE

MAX. / MIN. _____ °F / °C

PRECIPITATION

CONDITIONS

WIND

N NE E SE S SW W NW

TEMPERATURE

MAX. / MIN. _____ °F / °C

PRECIPITATION

CONDITIONS

WIND

N NE E SE S SW W NW

TEMPERATURE

MAX. / MIN. _____ °F / °C

PRECIPITATION

CONDITIONS

WIND

N NE E SE S SW W NW

MONDAY 14 | **TUESDAY 15** | **WEDNESDAY 16**

Flag Day

ROOT

FLOWER

LEAF

FLOWER

LEAF

ROOT

> Thin out tree fruit for
> heavier crops.
>
> Observe your fruit trees
> closely for pests
> and spray
> organically if necessary.
>
> Hang apple maggot traps
> now and keep them in
> place until harvest.

JUNE

M	T	W	T	F	S	S
	1	2	3	4	5	6
7	8	9	10	11	12	13
14	15	16	17	18	19	20
21	22	23	24	25	26	27
28	29	30				

TEMPERATURE

MAX./MIN. _____ °F /°C

PRECIPITATION

CONDITIONS

WIND

N NE E SE S SW W NW

TEMPERATURE

MAX./MIN. _____ °F /°C

PRECIPITATION

CONDITIONS

WIND

N NE E SE S SW W NW

TEMPERATURE

MAX./MIN. _____ °F /°C

PRECIPITATION

CONDITIONS

WIND

N NE E SE S SW W NW

THURSDAY 17 · FRIDAY 18 · SATURDAY 19

LEAF

FRUIT

FRUIT

SATURDAY 19

1 2 3 4 5 6 7 8 9 10 11 12
1 2 3 4 5 6 7 8 9 10 11 12

TEMPERATURE

MAX./MIN. _____ °F /°C

PRECIPITATION

CONDITIONS

WIND

N NE E SE S SW W NW

SUNDAY 20

Father's Day

ROOT

1 2 3 4 5 6 7 8 9 10 11 12
1 2 3 4 5 6 7 8 9 10 11 12

TEMPERATURE

MAX./MIN. _____ °F /°C

PRECIPITATION

CONDITIONS

WIND

N NE E SE S SW W NW

THURSDAY 17

TEMPERATURE

MAX./MIN. _____ °F /°C

PRECIPITATION

CONDITIONS

WIND

N NE E SE S SW W NW

FRIDAY 18

TEMPERATURE

MAX./MIN. _____ °F /°C

PRECIPITATION

CONDITIONS

WIND

N NE E SE S SW W NW

*Long about knee-deep in June,
'Bout the time
strawberries melts
On the vine*

JAMES WHITCOMB RILEY

*...nothing can bring back
the hour
Of splendour in the grass,
of glory in the flower.*

WILLIAM WORDSWORTH

In winter I get up at night
And dress by yellow
candlelight.
In summer,
quite the other way,
I have to go to bed by day.

ROBERT LOUIS STEVENSON

MONDAY **21**	TUESDAY **22**	WEDNESDAY **23**

The Longest Day of the Year:
Summer Begins

1
2
3
4
5
6
7
8
9
10
11
12
1
2
3
4
5
6
7
8
9
10
11
12

ROOT

ROOT

ROOT

Comes the longest light of
the year.

Build a small barbecue pit
for summer entertaining
or just for family use.
Many vegetables, and especially
summer squash, peppers,
corn, eggplant, and spring
onions, take on wonderfully
sweet and complex smoky
flavors when grilled.

FLOWER

JUNE

M	T	W	T	F	S	S
	1	2	3	4	5	6
7	8	9	10	11	12	13
14	15	16	17	18	19	20
21	22	23	24	25	26	27
28	29	30				

TEMPERATURE
MAX./MIN. _____ °F /°C
PRECIPITATION
CONDITIONS
WIND
N NE E SE S SW W NW

TEMPERATURE
MAX./MIN. _____ °F /°C
PRECIPITATION
CONDITIONS
WIND
N NE E SE S SW W NW

TEMPERATURE
MAX./MIN. _____ °F /°C
PRECIPITATION
CONDITIONS
WIND
N NE E SE S SW W NW

THURSDAY 24 **FRIDAY 25** **SATURDAY 26**

F L O W E R

F L O W E R

L E A F

1 2 3 4 5 6 7 8 9 10 11 12 1 2 3 4 5 6 7 8 9 10 11 12

TEMPERATURE

MAX./MIN. _____ °F /°C

PRECIPITATION

CONDITIONS

WIND

N NE E SE S SW W NW

SUNDAY 27

F L O W E R

L E A F

L E A F

1 2 3 4 5 6 7 8 9 10 11 12 1 2 3 4 5 6 7 8 9 10 11 12

Summer afternoon—summer afternoon; to me those have always been the two most beautiful words in the English language.

HENRY JAMES

(ATTRIB. BY EDITH WHARTON)

*Summertime
And the livin' is easy*

IRA GERSHWIN

TEMPERATURE

MAX./MIN. _____ °F /°C

PRECIPITATION

CONDITIONS

WIND

N NE E SE S SW W NW

TEMPERATURE

MAX./MIN. _____ °F /°C

PRECIPITATION

CONDITIONS

WIND

N NE E SE S SW W NW

TEMPERATURE

MAX./MIN. _____ °F /°C

PRECIPITATION

CONDITIONS

WIND

N NE E SE S SW W NW

J U N E   J U

| MONDAY **28** | TUESDAY **29** | WEDNESDAY **30** |

Replace short-season crops with a second planting. Try a new crop or a variety you've never tried before.

Control your insect population with beneficial insects, botanical extracts, or Bts (bacillus thurengenesis).

JULY

M	T	W	T	F	S	S
			1	2	3	4
5	6	7	8	9	10	11
12	13	14	15	16	17	18
19	20	21	22	23	24	25
26	27	28	29	30	31	

FRUIT

FRUIT

ROOT

TEMPERATURE
MAX./MIN._____ °F /°C
PRECIPITATION
CONDITIONS
WIND
N NE E SE S SW W NW

TEMPERATURE
MAX./MIN._____ °F /°C
PRECIPITATION
CONDITIONS
WIND
N NE E SE S SW W NW

TEMPERATURE
MAX./MIN._____ °F /°C
PRECIPITATION
CONDITIONS
WIND
N NE E SE S SW W NW

THURSDAY 1

Canada Day

FRIDAY 2

ROOT

SATURDAY 3

FLOWER

1 2 3 4 5 6 7 8 9 10 11 12 1 2 3 4 5 6 7 8 9 10 11 12

ROOT

TEMPERATURE

MAX./MIN. _____ °F /°C

PRECIPITATION

CONDITIONS

WIND

N NE E SE S SW W NW

SUNDAY 4

Independence Day

FLOWER

LEAF

1 2 3 4 5 6 7 8 9 10 11 12 1 2 3 4 5 6 7 8 9 10 11 12

FLOWER

ROOT

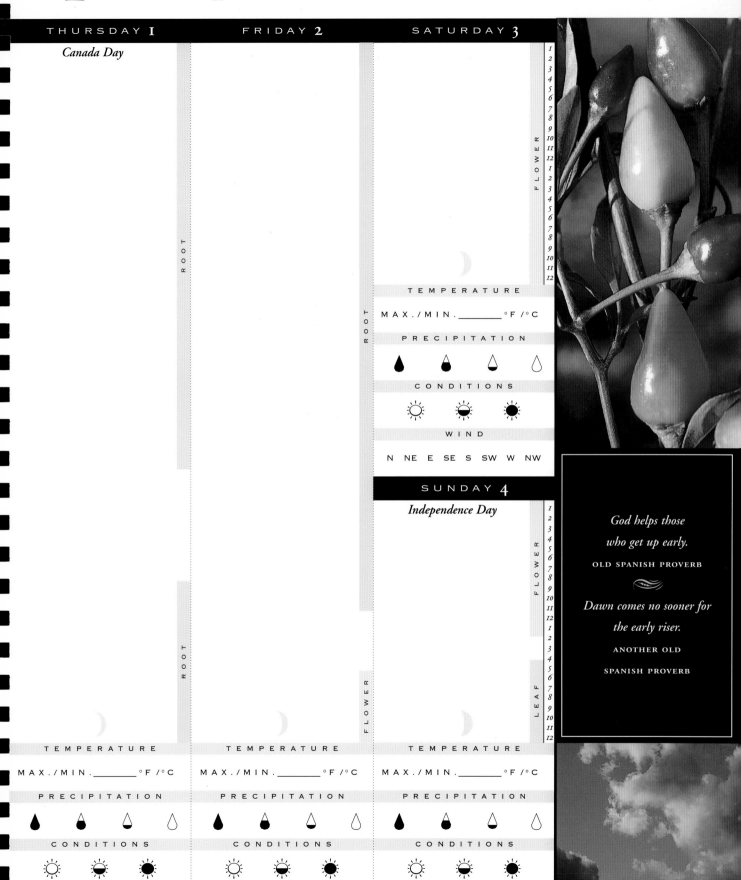

*God helps those
who get up early.*
OLD SPANISH PROVERB

*Dawn comes no sooner for
the early riser.*
ANOTHER OLD
SPANISH PROVERB

TEMPERATURE

MAX./MIN. _____ °F /°C

PRECIPITATION

CONDITIONS

WIND

N NE E SE S SW W NW

TEMPERATURE

MAX./MIN. _____ °F /°C

PRECIPITATION

CONDITIONS

WIND

N NE E SE S SW W NW

TEMPERATURE

MAX./MIN. _____ °F /°C

PRECIPITATION

CONDITIONS

WIND

N NE E SE S SW W NW

MONDAY 5 **TUESDAY 6** **WEDNESDAY 7**

*Use shade cloths
to protect your vegetables
from the blazing
summer sun.*

Expose the roots of your weeds.

*Review your composting habits
and make sure
you are recycling all the garden
and kitchen waste you can.*

JULY

M	T	W	T	F	S	S
			1	2	3	4
5	6	7	8	9	10	11
12	13	14	15	16	17	18
19	20	21	22	23	24	25
26	27	28	29	30	31	

LEAF

LEAF

FRUIT

1 2 3 4 5 6 7 8 9 10 11 12 1 2 3 4 5 6 7 8 9 10 11 12

TEMPERATURE

MAX./MIN. _____ °F /°C

PRECIPITATION

CONDITIONS

WIND

N NE E SE S SW W NW

TEMPERATURE

MAX./MIN. _____ °F /°C

PRECIPITATION

CONDITIONS

WIND

N NE E SE S SW W NW

TEMPERATURE

MAX./MIN. _____ °F /°C

PRECIPITATION

CONDITIONS

WIND

N NE E SE S SW W NW

THURSDAY 8

FRIDAY 9

SATURDAY 10

ROOT

1
2
3
4
5
6
7
8
9
10
11
12
1
2
3
4
5
6
7
8
9
10
11
12

TEMPERATURE

MAX./MIN. _____ °F /°C

PRECIPITATION

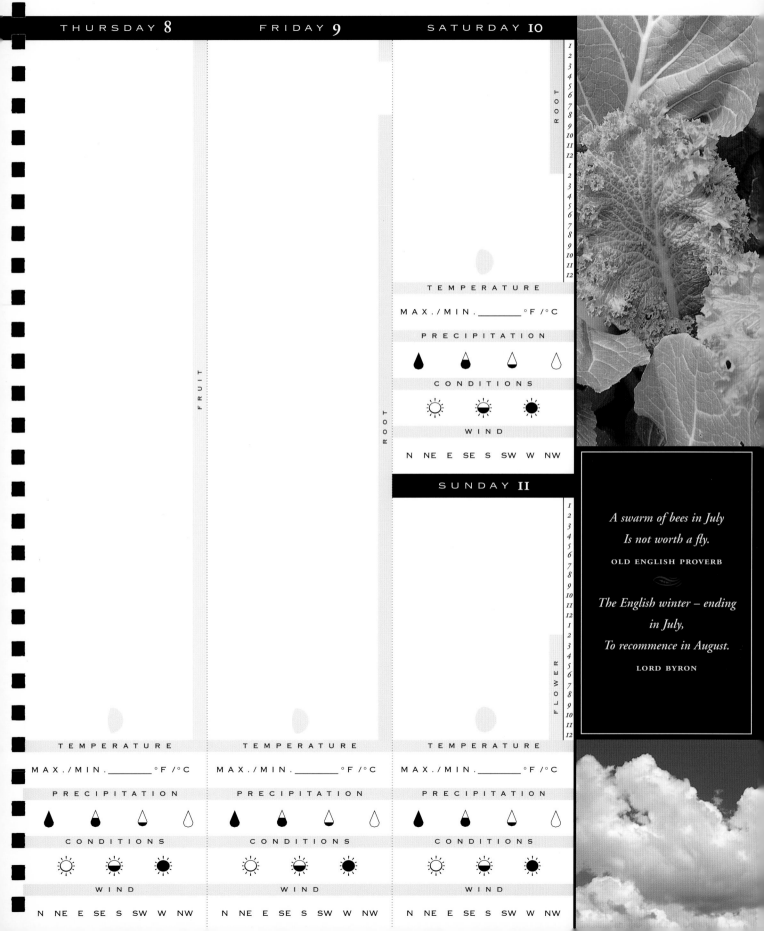

CONDITIONS

WIND

N NE E SE S SW W NW

SUNDAY 11

ROOT

FRUIT

FLOWER

1
2
3
4
5
6
7
8
9
10
11
12
1
2
3
4
5
6
7
8
9
10
11
12

TEMPERATURE

MAX./MIN. _____ °F /°C

PRECIPITATION

CONDITIONS

WIND

N NE E SE S SW W NW

TEMPERATURE

MAX./MIN. _____ °F /°C

PRECIPITATION

CONDITIONS

WIND

N NE E SE S SW W NW

TEMPERATURE

MAX./MIN. _____ °F /°C

PRECIPITATION

CONDITIONS

WIND

N NE E SE S SW W NW

*A swarm of bees in July
Is not worth a fly.*
OLD ENGLISH PROVERB

*The English winter – ending
in July,
To recommence in August.*
LORD BYRON

MONDAY 12 · **TUESDAY 13** · **WEDNESDAY 14**

FLOWER

FLOWER

LEAF

LEAF

FRUIT

*Do not be tempted
to apply synthetic fertilizer
or chemical herbicides
or insecticides.
Your plants and soil
are alive – at all costs
avoid killing beneficial insects
and microorganisms.*

JULY

M	T	W	T	F	S	S
			1	2	3	4
5	6	7	8	9	10	11
12	13	14	15	16	17	18
19	20	21	22	23	24	25
26	27	28	29	30	31	

1 2 3 4 5 6 7 8 9 10 11 12 1 2 3 4 5 6 7 8 9 10 11 12

TEMPERATURE

MAX./MIN. _____ °F /°C

PRECIPITATION

CONDITIONS

WIND

N NE E SE S SW W NW

TEMPERATURE

MAX./MIN. _____ °F /°C

PRECIPITATION

CONDITIONS

WIND

N NE E SE S SW W NW

TEMPERATURE

MAX./MIN. _____ °F /°C

PRECIPITATION

CONDITIONS

WIND

N NE E SE S SW W NW

THURSDAY 15

FRIDAY 16

SATURDAY 17

FRUIT

1
2
3
4
5
6
7
8
9
10
11
12

ROOT

1
2
3
4
5
6
7
8
9
10
11
12

FRUIT

TEMPERATURE

MAX./MIN. _____ °F /°C

PRECIPITATION

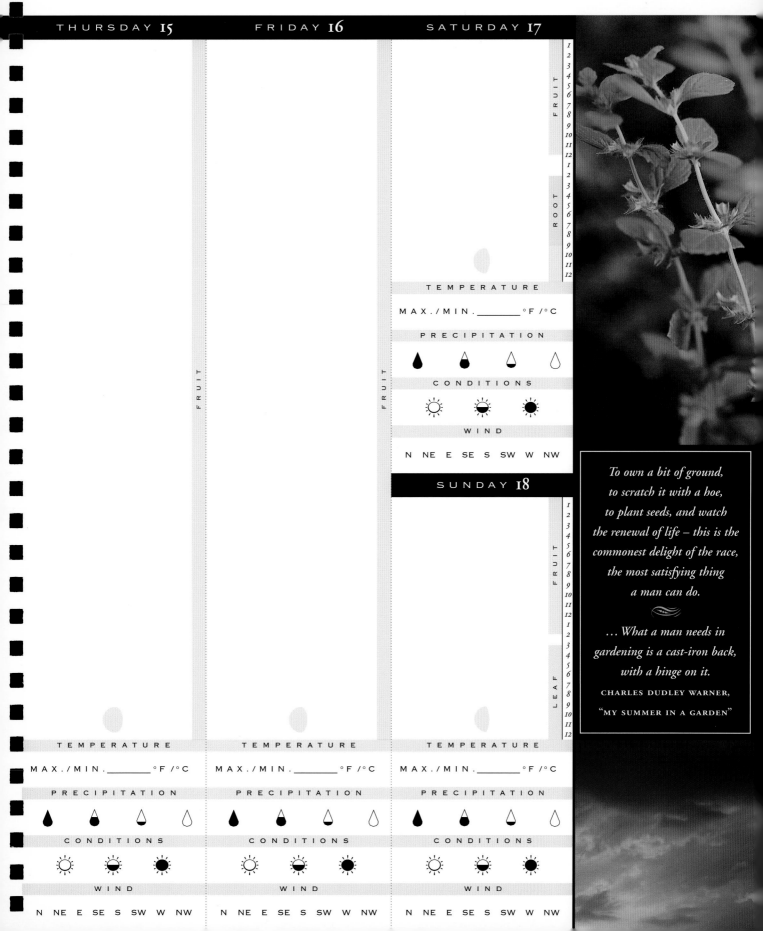

CONDITIONS

WIND

N NE E SE S SW W NW

SUNDAY 18

FRUIT

1
2
3
4
5
6
7
8
9
10
11
12

1
2
3
4
5
6
7
8

LEAF

9
10
11
12

FRUIT

> *To own a bit of ground,*
> *to scratch it with a hoe,*
> *to plant seeds, and watch*
> *the renewal of life – this is the*
> *commonest delight of the race,*
> *the most satisfying thing*
> *a man can do.*
>
> *… What a man needs in*
> *gardening is a cast-iron back,*
> *with a hinge on it.*
>
> CHARLES DUDLEY WARNER,
> "MY SUMMER IN A GARDEN"

TEMPERATURE

MAX./MIN. _____ °F /°C

PRECIPITATION

CONDITIONS

WIND

N NE E SE S SW W NW

TEMPERATURE

MAX./MIN. _____ °F /°C

PRECIPITATION

CONDITIONS

WIND

N NE E SE S SW W NW

TEMPERATURE

MAX./MIN. _____ °F /°C

PRECIPITATION

CONDITIONS

WIND

N NE E SE S SW W NW

MONDAY 19 **TUESDAY 20** **WEDNESDAY 21**

LEAF

ROOT

ROOT

FLOWER

> *Monitor your water usage
> and do everything you can
> in the home as well as
> the garden to conserve
> this precious resource.*
>
> *Put up a hammock or set out
> a comfortable garden chair
> and save some time to admire
> the burgeoning nature
> around you.*
> *Take in all the aromas and
> colors of your garden.*

JULY

M	T	W	T	F	S	S
			1	2	3	4
5	6	7	8	9	10	11
12	13	14	15	16	17	18
19	20	21	22	23	24	25
26	27	28	29	30	31	

1 2 3 4 5 6 7 8 9 10 11 12 1 2 3 4 5 6 7 8 9 10 11 12

TEMPERATURE

MAX./MIN. _____ °F /°C

PRECIPITATION

CONDITIONS

WIND

N NE E SE S SW W NW

TEMPERATURE

MAX./MIN. _____ °F /°C

PRECIPITATION

CONDITIONS

WIND

N NE E SE S SW W NW

TEMPERATURE

MAX./MIN. _____ °F /°C

PRECIPITATION

CONDITIONS

WIND

N NE E SE S SW W NW

THURSDAY 22

FRIDAY 23

SATURDAY 24

F L O W E R

L E A F

LEAF

1
2
3
4
5
6
7
8
9
10
11
12
1
2
3
4
5
6
7
8
9
10
11
12

TEMPERATURE

MAX./MIN. _____ °F /°C

PRECIPITATION

CONDITIONS

WIND

N NE E SE S SW W NW

SUNDAY 25

F R U I T

1
2
3
4
5
6
7
8
9
10
11
12
1
2
3
4
5
6
7
8
9
10
11
12

*Show me your garden, and I
shall tell you what you are.*

ALFRED AUSTIN,
"THE GARDEN THAT I LOVE"

*The whole world is a garden,
and what a wonderful place
this would be, if only each of
us took care of our part of
the Garden!*

VOLTAIRE

TEMPERATURE

MAX./MIN. _____ °F /°C

PRECIPITATION

CONDITIONS

WIND

N NE E SE S SW W NW

TEMPERATURE

MAX./MIN. _____ °F /°C

PRECIPITATION

CONDITIONS

WIND

N NE E SE S SW W NW

TEMPERATURE

MAX./MIN. _____ °F /°C

PRECIPITATION

CONDITIONS

WIND

N NE E SE S SW W NW

MONDAY 26

TUESDAY 27

WEDNESDAY 28

Pick your vegetables in the early morning before the sun evaporates their moisture.

Use silver or colored strips of tape to scare birds from your ripening fruit.

FRUIT

FRUIT

ROOT

JULY

M	T	W	T	F	S	S
			1	2	3	4
5	6	7	8	9	10	11
12	13	14	15	16	17	18
19	20	21	22	23	24	25
26	27	28	29	30	31	

1
2
3
4
5
6
7
8
9
10
11
12
1
2
3
4
5
6
7
8
9
10
11
12

TEMPERATURE

MAX./MIN. _____ °F /°C

PRECIPITATION

CONDITIONS

WIND

N NE E SE S SW W NW

TEMPERATURE

MAX./MIN. _____ °F /°C

PRECIPITATION

CONDITIONS

WIND

N NE E SE S SW W NW

TEMPERATURE

MAX./MIN. _____ °F /°C

PRECIPITATION

CONDITIONS

WIND

N NE E SE S SW W NW

THURSDAY **29**

FRIDAY **30**

SATURDAY **31**

LEAF

FLOWER

ROOT

FLOWER

LEAF

LEAF

1 2 3 4 5 6 7 8 9 10 11 12 1 2 3 4 5 6 7 8 9 10 11 12

TEMPERATURE

MAX./MIN. _____ °F /°C

PRECIPITATION

CONDITIONS

WIND

N NE E SE S SW W NW

SUNDAY **1**

1 2 3 4 5 6 7 8 9 10 11 12 1 2 3 4 5 6 7 8 9 10 11 12

Here's flowers for you:
Hot lavender, mints, savory,
marjoram,
The marigold, that goes to
bed wi' the sun,
And with him rises weeping:
these are the flowers
Of middle summer, and I
think they are given
To men of middle age.

WILLIAM SHAKESPEARE

TEMPERATURE

MAX./MIN. _____ °F /°C

PRECIPITATION

CONDITIONS

WIND

N NE E SE S SW W NW

TEMPERATURE

MAX./MIN. _____ °F /°C

PRECIPITATION

CONDITIONS

WIND

N NE E SE S SW W NW

TEMPERATURE

MAX./MIN. _____ °F /°C

PRECIPITATION

CONDITIONS

WIND

N NE E SE S SW W NW

MONDAY 2 | **TUESDAY 3** | **WEDNESDAY 4**

1
2
3
4
5
6
7
8
9
10
11
12
1
2
3
4
5
6
7
8
9
10
11
12

LEAF

LEAF

FRUIT

FRUIT

*Keep pruning old roses
to encourage
leaf and flower production.*

*Collect all "windfall" tree fruit
to interrupt the life cycle
of harmful pests that might
lie inside.*

AUGUST

M	T	W	T	F	S	S
						1
2	3	4	5	6	7	8
9	10	11	12	13	14	15
16	17	18	19	20	21	22
23/30	24/31	25	26	27	28	29

TEMPERATURE | TEMPERATURE | TEMPERATURE

MAX./MIN. _____ °F /°C | MAX./MIN. _____ °F /°C | MAX./MIN. _____ °F /°C

PRECIPITATION | PRECIPITATION | PRECIPITATION

CONDITIONS | CONDITIONS | CONDITIONS

WIND | WIND | WIND

N NE E SE S SW W NW | N NE E SE S SW W NW | N NE E SE S SW W NW

THURSDAY **5**

FRIDAY **6**

SATURDAY **7**

ROOT

1 2 3 4 5 6 7 8 9 10 11 12 1 2 3 4 5 6 7 8 9 10 11 12

FRUIT

ROOT

ROOT

TEMPERATURE

MAX./MIN. _____ °F /°C

PRECIPITATION

CONDITIONS

WIND

N NE E SE S SW W NW

SUNDAY **8**

FLOWER

1 2 3 4 5 6 7 8 9 10 11 12 1 2 3 4 5 6 7 8 9 10 11 12

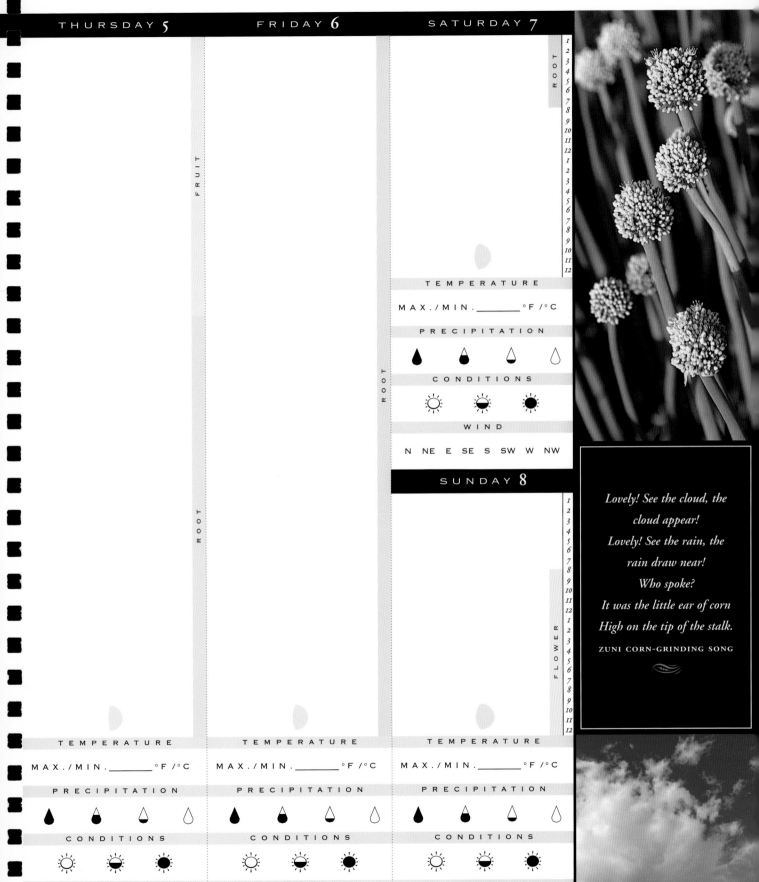

Lovely! See the cloud, the
cloud appear!
Lovely! See the rain, the
rain draw near!
Who spoke?
It was the little ear of corn
High on the tip of the stalk.
ZUNI CORN-GRINDING SONG

TEMPERATURE

MAX./MIN. _____ °F /°C

PRECIPITATION

CONDITIONS

WIND

N NE E SE S SW W NW

TEMPERATURE

MAX./MIN. _____ °F /°C

PRECIPITATION

CONDITIONS

WIND

N NE E SE S SW W NW

TEMPERATURE

MAX./MIN. _____ °F /°C

PRECIPITATION

CONDITIONS

WIND

N NE E SE S SW W NW

MONDAY 9

TUESDAY 10

WEDNESDAY 11

Blackberries, peaches, plums,
apples, tomatoes, corn,
and summer squash
are all now in peak season.

Water and weed as necessary
to keep your crops thriving.
Watering is best done
early in the morning
to give the water
time to soak into the soil
before the sun evaporates it.

AUGUST

M	T	W	T	F	S	S
						1
2	*3*	*4*	*5*	*6*	*7*	*8*
9	*10*	*11*	*12*	*13*	*14*	*15*
16	*17*	*18*	*19*	*20*	*21*	*22*
23/30	*24/31*	*25*	*26*	*27*	*28*	*29*

FLOWER

LEAF

LEAF

FRUIT

TEMPERATURE

MAX./MIN. _____ °F /°C

PRECIPITATION

CONDITIONS

WIND

N NE E SE S SW W NW

TEMPERATURE

MAX./MIN. _____ °F /°C

PRECIPITATION

CONDITIONS

WIND

N NE E SE S SW W NW

TEMPERATURE

MAX./MIN. _____ °F /°C

PRECIPITATION

CONDITIONS

WIND

N NE E SE S SW W NW

THURSDAY 12

FRIDAY 13

SATURDAY 14

FRUIT

ROOT

1
2
3
4
5
6
7
8
9
10
11
12
1
2
3
4
5
6
7
8
9
10
11
12

FRUIT

TEMPERATURE

MAX./MIN. _____ °F /°C

PRECIPITATION

CONDITIONS

WIND

N   NE   E   SE   S   SW   W   NW

SUNDAY 15

ROOT

1
2
3
4
5
6
7
8
9
10
11
12
1
2
3
4
5
6
7
8
9
10
11
12

The thirsty earth soaks up
the rain,
And drinks, and gapes for
drink again.
The plants suck in the earth,
and are
With constant drinking fresh
and fair.

ABRAHAM COWLEY

TEMPERATURE

MAX./MIN. _____ °F /°C

PRECIPITATION

CONDITIONS

WIND

N   NE   E   SE   S   SW   W   NW

TEMPERATURE

MAX./MIN. _____ °F /°C

PRECIPITATION

CONDITIONS

WIND

N   NE   E   SE   S   SW   W   NW

TEMPERATURE

MAX./MIN. _____ °F /°C

PRECIPITATION

CONDITIONS

WIND

N   NE   E   SE   S   SW   W   NW

MONDAY 16	TUESDAY 17	WEDNESDAY 18

*Water the garden by hand
as much as possible
to avoid overwatering
and unnecessary runoff.
Learn which plants
need more or less moisture.*

*Water at intervals
for best results;
leave at least one day
between waterings.*

AUGUST

M	T	W	T	F	S	S
						I
2	3	4	5	6	7	8
9	I0	II	I2	I3	I4	I5
I6	I7	I8	I9	20	2I	22
23/30	24/31	25	26	27	28	29

ROOT

FLOWER

ROOT

LEAF

FLOWER

TEMPERATURE	TEMPERATURE	TEMPERATURE
MAX./MIN. _____ °F /°C	MAX./MIN. _____ °F /°C	MAX./MIN. _____ °F /°C
PRECIPITATION	PRECIPITATION	PRECIPITATION
CONDITIONS	CONDITIONS	CONDITIONS
WIND	WIND	WIND
N NE E SE S SW W NW	N NE E SE S SW W NW	N NE E SE S SW W NW

THURSDAY 19

FRIDAY 20

SATURDAY 21

LEAF

FRUIT

1 2 3 4 5 6 7 8 9 10 11 12
1 2 3 4 5 6 7 8 9 10 11 12

TEMPERATURE

MAX./MIN. _____ °F /°C

PRECIPITATION

CONDITIONS

WIND

N NE E SE S SW W NW

SUNDAY 22

LEAF

FRUIT

1 2 3 4 5 6 7 8 9 10 11 12
1 2 3 4 5 6 7 8 9 10 11 12

LEAF

LEAF

LEAF

TEMPERATURE

MAX./MIN. _____ °F /°C

PRECIPITATION

CONDITIONS

WIND

N NE E SE S SW W NW

TEMPERATURE

MAX./MIN. _____ °F /°C

PRECIPITATION

CONDITIONS

WIND

N NE E SE S SW W NW

TEMPERATURE

MAX./MIN. _____ °F /°C

PRECIPITATION

CONDITIONS

WIND

N NE E SE S SW W NW

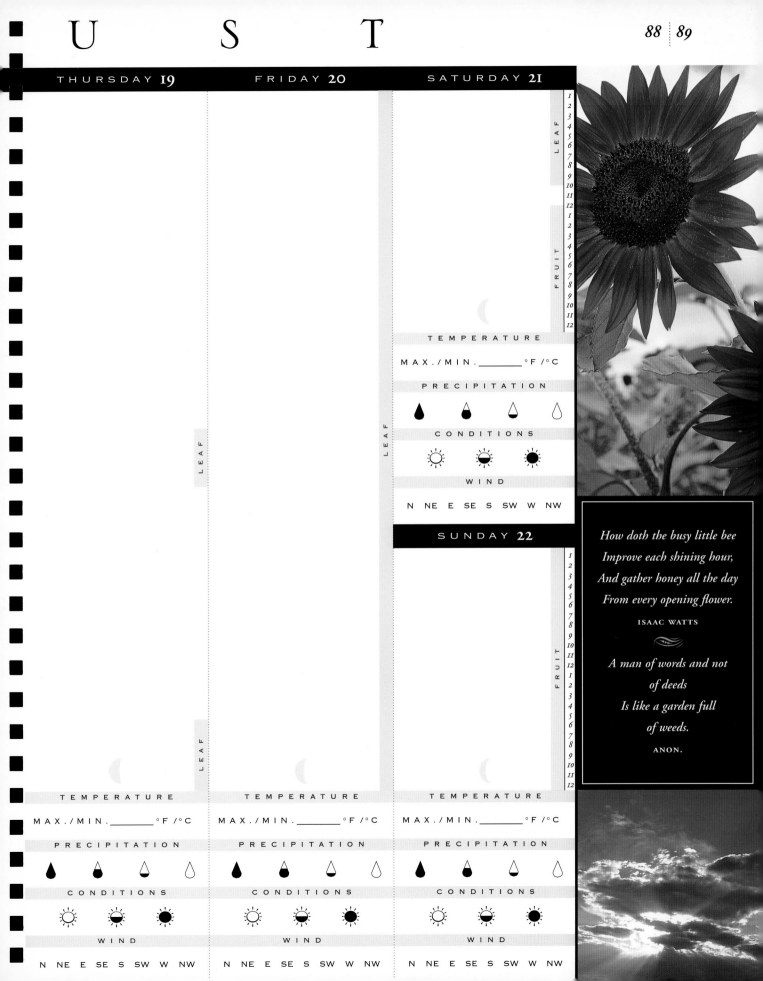

How doth the busy little bee
Improve each shining hour,
And gather honey all the day
From every opening flower.

ISAAC WATTS

A man of words and not
of deeds
Is like a garden full
of weeds.

ANON.

The height of summer represents the symphony of your gardening efforts.

Weed for the final time and begin preparations for the fall garden.

Turn your compost.

AUGUST

M	T	W	T	F	S	S
						I
2	3	4	5	6	7	8
9	10	11	12	13	14	15
16	17	18	19	20	21	22
23/30	24/31	25	26	27	28	29

MONDAY 23

FRUIT

TUESDAY 24

FRUIT

ROOT

WEDNESDAY 25

ROOT

ROOT

TEMPERATURE
MAX./MIN. _____ °F /°C
PRECIPITATION
CONDITIONS
WIND
N NE E SE S SW W NW

TEMPERATURE
MAX./MIN. _____ °F /°C
PRECIPITATION
CONDITIONS
WIND
N NE E SE S SW W NW

TEMPERATURE
MAX./MIN. _____ °F /°C
PRECIPITATION
CONDITIONS
WIND
N NE E SE S SW W NW

THURSDAY 26

FRIDAY 27

SATURDAY 28

ROOT

FRUIT

LEAF

1
2
3
4
5
6
7
8
9
10
11
12
1
2
3
4
5
6
7
8
9
10
11
12

TEMPERATURE

MAX./MIN. _____ °F /°C

PRECIPITATION

CONDITIONS

WIND

N NE E SE S SW W NW

FLOWER

SUNDAY 29

LEAF

1
2
3
4
5
6
7
8
9
10
11
12
1
2
3
4
5
6
7
8
9
10
11
12

FLOWER

TEMPERATURE

MAX./MIN. _____ °F /°C

PRECIPITATION

CONDITIONS

WIND

N NE E SE S SW W NW

TEMPERATURE

MAX./MIN. _____ °F /°C

PRECIPITATION

CONDITIONS

WIND

N NE E SE S SW W NW

TEMPERATURE

MAX./MIN. _____ °F /°C

PRECIPITATION

CONDITIONS

WIND

N NE E SE S SW W NW

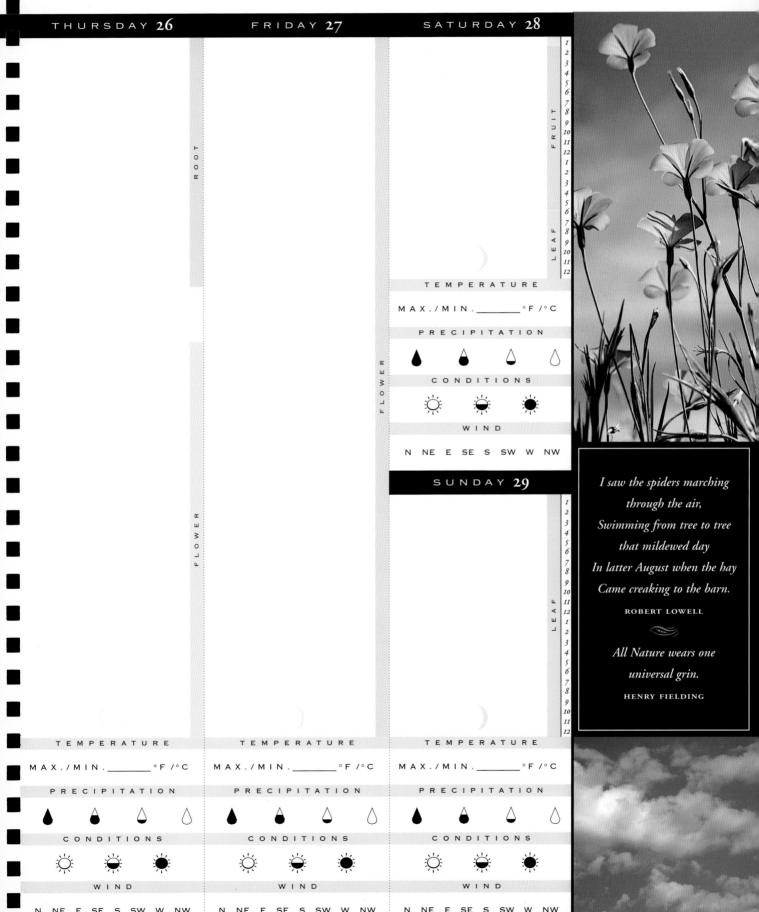

*I saw the spiders marching
through the air,
Swimming from tree to tree
that mildewed day
In latter August when the hay
Came creaking to the barn.*

ROBERT LOWELL

*All Nature wears one
universal grin.*

HENRY FIELDING

MONDAY 30

TUESDAY 31

WEDNESDAY 1

Harvest, harvest, harvest!

*Be sure to keep notes
on yields and which plants
have done well
in which locations.*

*Assess your garden's strengths
and weaknesses.*

SEPTEMBER

M	T	W	T	F	S	S
		1	2	3	4	5
6	7	8	9	10	11	12
13	14	15	16	17	18	19
20	21	22	23	24	25	26
27	28	29	30			

LEAF

FRUIT

FRUIT

FRUIT

ROOT

1 2 3 4 5 6 7 8 9 10 11 12 1 2 3 4 5 6 7 8 9 10 11 12

TEMPERATURE
MAX./MIN. _____ °F /°C
PRECIPITATION
CONDITIONS
WIND
N NE E SE S SW W NW

TEMPERATURE
MAX./MIN. _____ °F /°C
PRECIPITATION
CONDITIONS
WIND
N NE E SE S SW W NW

TEMPERATURE
MAX./MIN. _____ °F /°C
PRECIPITATION
CONDITIONS
WIND
N NE E SE S SW W NW

THURSDAY 2

FRIDAY 3

SATURDAY 4

FRUIT

FLOWER

1 2 3 4 5 6 7 8 9 10 11 12 1 2 3 4 5 6 7 8 9 10 11 12

TEMPERATURE

MAX./MIN. _____ °F/°C

PRECIPITATION

CONDITIONS

WIND

ROOT

N NE E SE S SW W NW

SUNDAY 5

FLOWER

1 2 3 4 5 6 7 8 9 10 11 12 1 2 3 4 5 6 7 8 9 10 11 12

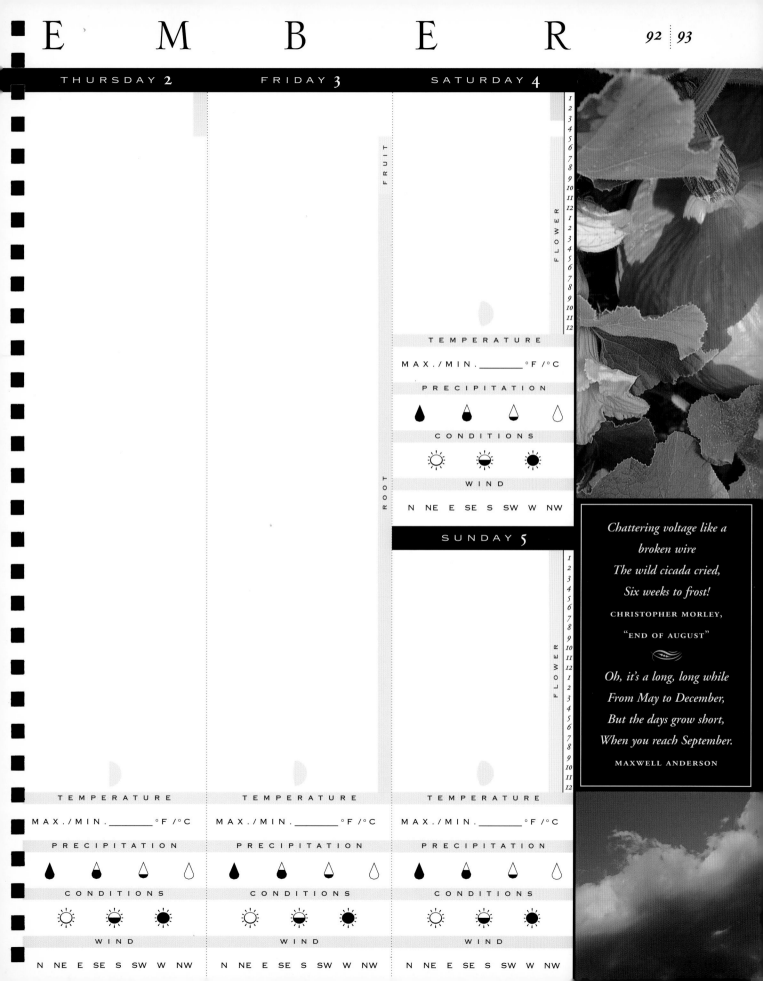

*Chattering voltage like a
broken wire
The wild cicada cried,
Six weeks to frost!*
CHRISTOPHER MORLEY,
"END OF AUGUST"

*Oh, it's a long, long while
From May to December,
But the days grow short,
When you reach September.*
MAXWELL ANDERSON

TEMPERATURE

MAX./MIN. _____ °F/°C

PRECIPITATION

CONDITIONS

WIND

N NE E SE S SW W NW

TEMPERATURE

MAX./MIN. _____ °F/°C

PRECIPITATION

CONDITIONS

WIND

N NE E SE S SW W NW

TEMPERATURE

MAX./MIN. _____ °F/°C

PRECIPITATION

CONDITIONS

WIND

N NE E SE S SW W NW

MONDAY 6

Labor Day

FLOWER

LEAF

TUESDAY 7

LEAF

LEAF

FRUIT

WEDNESDAY 8

FRUIT

*Rejoice in your work.
Remember – the richness
of life is
in your hands.*

*Encourage your family
to help in the garden,
picking crops and keeping
things tidy.
Instill a love of nature
in your children.*

SEPTEMBER

M	T	W	T	F	S	S
		1	2	3	4	5
6	7	8	9	10	11	12
13	14	15	16	17	18	19
20	21	22	23	24	25	26
27	28	29	30			

1 2 3 4 5 6 7 8 9 10 11 12 1 2 3 4 5 6 7 8 9 10 11 12

TEMPERATURE

MAX./MIN. _____ °F /°C

PRECIPITATION

CONDITIONS

WIND

N NE E SE S SW W NW

TEMPERATURE

MAX./MIN. _____ °F /°C

PRECIPITATION

CONDITIONS

WIND

N NE E SE S SW W NW

TEMPERATURE

MAX./MIN. _____ °F /°C

PRECIPITATION

CONDITIONS

WIND

N NE E SE S SW W NW

THURSDAY 9

FRIDAY 10

SATURDAY 11

Rosh Hashanah
(Jewish New Year)

FRUIT

ROOT

1 2 3 4 5 6 7 8 9 10 11 12 1 2 3 4 5 6 7 8 9 10 11 12

TEMPERATURE

MAX./MIN. _____ °F / °C

PRECIPITATION

CONDITIONS

WIND

N   NE   E   SE   S   SW   W   NW

SUNDAY 12

ROOT

1 2 3 4 5 6 7 8 9 10 11 12 1 2 3 4 5 6 7 8 9 10 11 12

FRUIT

ROOT

No man but feels more of a man in the world if he have a bit of ground that he can call his own. However small it is on the surface, it is four thousand miles deep; and that is a very handsome property.

CHARLES DUDLEY WARNER,
"MY SUMMER IN A GARDEN"

TEMPERATURE

MAX./MIN. _____ °F / °C

PRECIPITATION

CONDITIONS

WIND

N   NE   E   SE   S   SW   W   NW

TEMPERATURE

MAX./MIN. _____ °F / °C

PRECIPITATION

CONDITIONS

WIND

N   NE   E   SE   S   SW   W   NW

TEMPERATURE

MAX./MIN. _____ °F / °C

PRECIPITATION

CONDITIONS

WIND

N   NE   E   SE   S   SW   W   NW

MONDAY 13	TUESDAY 14	WEDNESDAY 15

Grapes, apples, pears, and onions are in abundance now.

Save the best seeds from your best plants and prepare the drying and storing processes.

Prepare cloches: simple frost covers with frames and clear plastic.

ROOT

ROOT

ROOT

LEAF

SEPTEMBER

M	T	W	T	F	S	S
		1	2	3	4	5
6	7	8	9	10	11	12
13	14	15	16	17	18	19
20	21	22	23	24	25	26
27	28	29	30			

1
2
3
4
5
6
7
8
9
10
11
12
1
2
3
4
5
6
7
8
9
10
11
12

TEMPERATURE

MAX./MIN. _____ °F /°C

PRECIPITATION

CONDITIONS

WIND

N NE E SE S SW W NW

TEMPERATURE

MAX./MIN. _____ °F /°C

PRECIPITATION

CONDITIONS

WIND

N NE E SE S SW W NW

TEMPERATURE

MAX./MIN. _____ °F /°C

PRECIPITATION

CONDITIONS

WIND

N NE E SE S SW W NW

THURSDAY 16

LEAF

FRIDAY 17

ROOT

LEAF

SATURDAY 18

FRUIT

1 2 3 4 5 6 7 8 9 10 11 12 1 2 3 4 5 6 7 8 9 10 11 12

TEMPERATURE

MAX./MIN._____°F /°C

PRECIPITATION

CONDITIONS

WIND

N NE E SE S SW W NW

SUNDAY 19

1 2 3 4 5 6 7 8 9 10 11 12 1 2 3 4 5 6 7 8 9 10 11 12

FRUIT

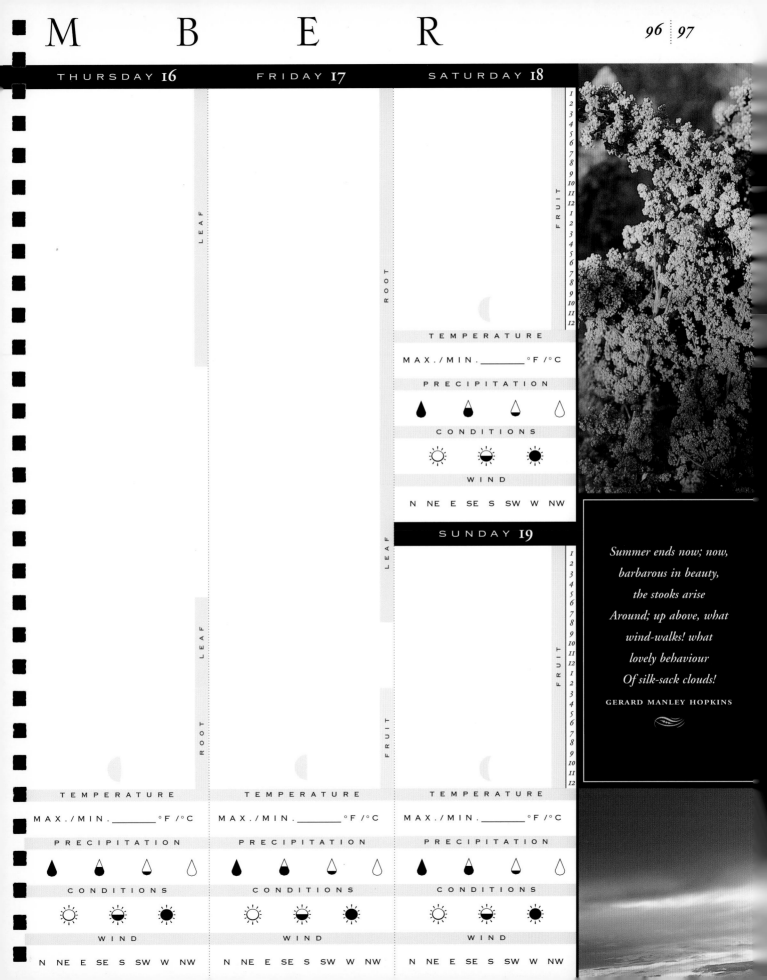

> Summer ends now; now,
> barbarous in beauty,
> the stooks arise
> Around; up above, what
> wind-walks! what
> lovely behaviour
> Of silk-sack clouds!
>
> GERARD MANLEY HOPKINS

LEAF

ROOT

LEAF

FRUIT

TEMPERATURE

MAX./MIN._____°F /°C

PRECIPITATION

CONDITIONS

WIND

N NE E SE S SW W NW

TEMPERATURE

MAX./MIN._____°F /°C

PRECIPITATION

CONDITIONS

WIND

N NE E SE S SW W NW

TEMPERATURE

MAX./MIN._____°F /°C

PRECIPITATION

CONDITIONS

WIND

N NE E SE S SW W NW

*Seasons of mists
and mellow fruitfulness,
Close bosom-friend of
the maturing sun.*

JOHN KEATS, "TO AUTUMN"

MONDAY **20**	TUESDAY **21**	WEDNESDAY **22**

Yom Kippur

FRUIT — ROOT — ROOT

*Plant your
overwintering crops.*

*Dig holes for planting trees
in the fall now,
taking care to generously water
the holes in advance
of planting and to add
cured compost.*

*Celebrate the autumn
equinox.*

SEPTEMBER

M	T	W	T	F	S	S
	1	*2*	*3*	*4*	*5*
6	*7*	*8*	*9*	*10*	*11*	*12*
13	*14*	*15*	*16*	*17*	*18*	*19*
20	*21*	*22*	*23*	*24*	*25*	*26*
27	*28*	*29*	*30*			

ROOT — ROOT — FLOWER

TEMPERATURE

MAX./MIN. _____ °F /°C

PRECIPITATION

CONDITIONS

WIND

N NE E SE S SW W NW

TEMPERATURE

MAX./MIN. _____ °F /°C

PRECIPITATION

CONDITIONS

WIND

N NE E SE S SW W NW

TEMPERATURE

MAX./MIN. _____ °F /°C

PRECIPITATION

CONDITIONS

WIND

N NE E SE S SW W NW

THURSDAY 23

Fall Begins

FLOWER

ROOT

TEMPERATURE

MAX./MIN. _____ °F /°C

PRECIPITATION

CONDITIONS

WIND

N NE E SE S SW W NW

FRIDAY 24

ROOT

FLOWER

ROOT

TEMPERATURE

MAX./MIN. _____ °F /°C

PRECIPITATION

CONDITIONS

WIND

N NE E SE S SW W NW

SATURDAY 25

ROOT
1
2
3
4
5
6
7
8
9
10
11
12

LEAF
1
2
3
4
5
6
7
8
9
10
11
12

TEMPERATURE

MAX./MIN. _____ °F /°C

PRECIPITATION

CONDITIONS

WIND

N NE E SE S SW W NW

SUNDAY 26

ROOT
1
2
3
4
5
6
7
8
9
10
11
12
1
2
3
4
5
6
7
8
9

LEAF
10
11
12

TEMPERATURE

MAX./MIN. _____ °F /°C

PRECIPITATION

CONDITIONS

WIND

N NE E SE S SW W NW

> Up from the meadows rich
> with corn,
> Clear in the cool September
> morn.
>
> JOHN GREENLEAF WHITTIER
>
> The physician can bury
> his mistakes, but the architect
> can only advise his client
> to plant vines.
>
> FRANK LLOYD WRIGHT

MONDAY 27   **TUESDAY 28**   **WEDNESDAY 29**

*Plant cover crops to fix
nitrogen in the soil and to
provide carbonaceous material
for compost.
Try to keep half of the garden
in annual, biennial,
or perennial cover crops.*

SEPTEMBER

M	T	W	T	F	S	S
		1	2	3	4	5
6	7	8	9	10	11	12
13	14	15	16	17	18	19
20	21	22	23	24	25	26
27	28	29	30			

1 2 3 4 5 6 7 8 9 10 11 12 1 2 3 4 5 6 7 8 9 10 11 12

LEAF

FRUIT

ROOT

TEMPERATURE

MAX./MIN. _____ °F /°C

PRECIPITATION

CONDITIONS

WIND

N NE E SE S SW W NW

TEMPERATURE

MAX./MIN. _____ °F /°C

PRECIPITATION

CONDITIONS

WIND

N NE E SE S SW W NW

TEMPERATURE

MAX./MIN. _____ °F /°C

PRECIPITATION

CONDITIONS

WIND

N NE E SE S SW W NW

THURSDAY 30	FRIDAY 1	SATURDAY 2

ROOT

ROOT

FLOWER

1 2 3 4 5 6 7 8 9 10 11 12

TEMPERATURE

MAX./MIN. _____ °F /°C

PRECIPITATION

CONDITIONS

WIND

N NE E SE S SW W NW

SUNDAY 3

FLOWER

FLOWER

LEAF

1 2 3 4 5 6 7 8 9 10 11 12

Crown'd with the sickle, and
the wheaten sheaf,
While Autumn, nodding o'er
the yellow plain,
Comes jovial on.
JAMES THOMSON

He that plants trees loves
others beside himself.
THOMAS FULLER

TEMPERATURE

MAX./MIN. _____ °F /°C

PRECIPITATION

CONDITIONS

WIND

N NE E SE S SW W NW

TEMPERATURE

MAX./MIN. _____ °F /°C

PRECIPITATION

CONDITIONS

WIND

N NE E SE S SW W NW

TEMPERATURE

MAX./MIN. _____ °F /°C

PRECIPITATION

CONDITIONS

WIND

N NE E SE S SW W NW

MONDAY 4	TUESDAY 5	WEDNESDAY 6

To limit the effects of sudden early light frost, spray your plants and trees with water.

❧

Persimmon season; and harvest time for grapes and kiwi fruit.

❧

Plant your indoor hyacinth bulbs.

OCTOBER

M	T	W	T	F	S	S
			1	2	3
4	5	6	7	8	9	10
11	12	13	14	15	16	17
18	19	20	21	22	23	24
25	26	27	28	29	30	31

LEAF

FRUIT

LEAF

FRUIT

ROOT

FRUIT

TEMPERATURE

MAX./MIN. _____ °F /°C

PRECIPITATION

CONDITIONS

WIND

N NE E SE S SW W NW

TEMPERATURE

MAX./MIN. _____ °F /°C

PRECIPITATION

CONDITIONS

WIND

N NE E SE S SW W NW

TEMPERATURE

MAX./MIN. _____ °F /°C

PRECIPITATION

CONDITIONS

WIND

N NE E SE S SW W NW

THURSDAY 7

FRUIT

ROOT

TEMPERATURE

MAX./MIN. _____ °F / °C

PRECIPITATION

CONDITIONS

WIND

N NE E SE S SW W NW

FRIDAY 8

FRUIT

ROOT

TEMPERATURE

MAX./MIN. _____ °F / °C

PRECIPITATION

CONDITIONS

WIND

N NE E SE S SW W NW

SATURDAY 9

ROOT

FRUIT

1
2
3
4
5
6
7
8
9
10
11
12
1
2
3
4
5
6
7
8
9
10
11
12

TEMPERATURE

MAX./MIN. _____ °F / °C

PRECIPITATION

CONDITIONS

WIND

N NE E SE S SW W NW

SUNDAY 10

ROOT

1
2
3
4
5
6
7
8
9
10
11
12
1
2
3
4
5
6
7
8
9
10
11
12

TEMPERATURE

MAX./MIN. _____ °F / °C

PRECIPITATION

CONDITIONS

WIND

N NE E SE S SW W NW

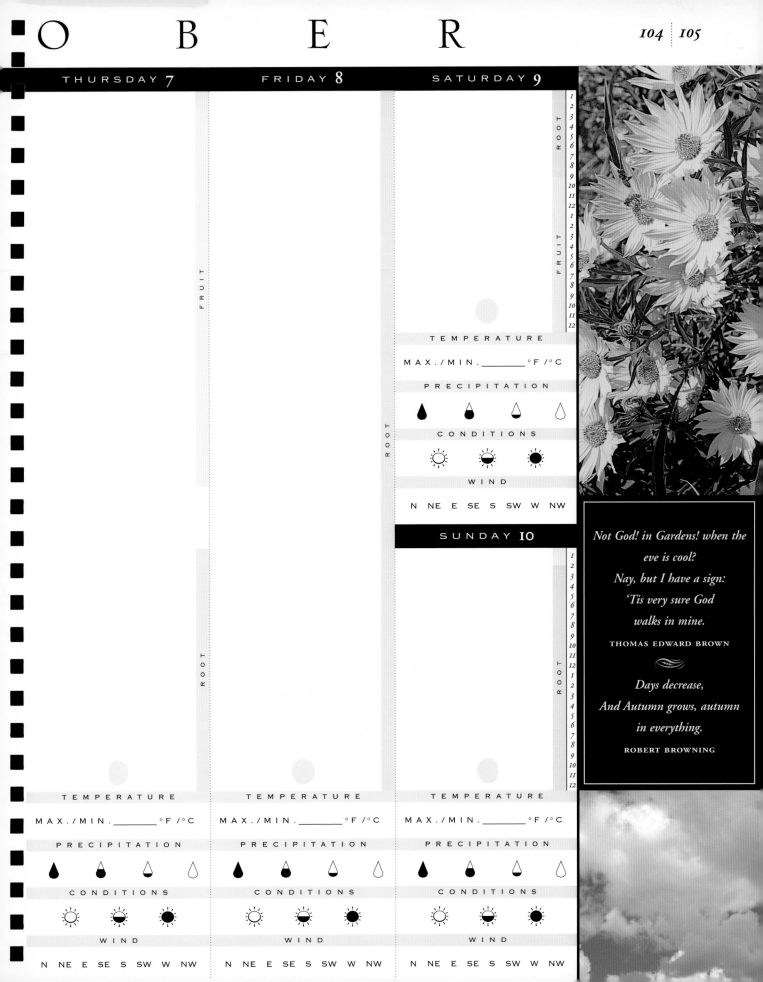

*Not God! in Gardens! when the
eve is cool?
Nay, but I have a sign:
'Tis very sure God
walks in mine.*

THOMAS EDWARD BROWN

*Days decrease,
And Autumn grows, autumn
in everything.*

ROBERT BROWNING

O C T

| MONDAY **II** | TUESDAY **I2** | WEDNESDAY **I3** |

Columbus Day (Observed)
Thanksgiving Day (Canada)

I
2
3
4
5
6
7
8
9
I0
II
I2
I
2
3
4
5
6
7
8
9
I0
II
I2

FLOWER

FLOWER

LEAF

If you're concerned about the first frost killing your prized plants, take cuttings and root them in water on a sunny windowsill indoors.

Autumn leaves on the lawn? Mow them and leave them as valuable composting mulch for your grass, or transfer them to your compost pile.

OCTOBER

M	T	W	T	F	S	S
			I	2	3	
4	5	6	7	8	9	I0
II	I2	I3	I4	I5	I6	I7
I8	I9	20	2I	22	23	24
25	26	27	28	29	30	3I

TEMPERATURE

MAX./MIN._____°F /°C

PRECIPITATION

CONDITIONS

WIND

N NE E SE S SW W NW

TEMPERATURE

MAX./MIN._____°F /°C

PRECIPITATION

CONDITIONS

WIND

N NE E SE S SW W NW

TEMPERATURE

MAX./MIN._____°F /°C

PRECIPITATION

CONDITIONS

WIND

N NE E SE S SW W NW

THURSDAY 14

LEAF

FRIDAY 15

LEAF

SATURDAY 16

FRUIT

1
2
3
4
5
6
7
8
9
10
11
12
1
2
3
4
5
6
7
8
9
10
11
12

TEMPERATURE

MAX./MIN._____°F /°C

PRECIPITATION

CONDITIONS

WIND

N NE E SE S SW W NW

SUNDAY 17

FRUIT

1
2
3
4
5
6
7
8
9
10
11
12
1
2
3
4
5
6
7
8
9
10
11
12

*Listen! the wind is rising,
and the air is wild with leaves,
We have had our
summer evenings,
now for October eves!*

HUMBERT WOLFE

TEMPERATURE

MAX./MIN._____°F /°C

PRECIPITATION

CONDITIONS

WIND

N NE E SE S SW W NW

TEMPERATURE

MAX./MIN._____°F /°C

PRECIPITATION

CONDITIONS

WIND

N NE E SE S SW W NW

TEMPERATURE

MAX./MIN._____°F /°C

PRECIPITATION

CONDITIONS

WIND

N NE E SE S SW W NW

MONDAY 18 **TUESDAY 19** **WEDNESDAY 20**

ROOT

*Plant late green manure
winter cover crops such as
winter rye.*

*Harvest root vegetables
as late as possible in the fall:
the cool ground is likely to be
the best place for them.*

OCTOBER

M	T	W	T	F	S	S
			I	2	3
4	5	6	7	8	9	10
II	I2	I3	I4	I5	I6	I7
I8	I9	20	2I	22	23	24
25	26	27	28	29	30	3I

I
2
3
4
5
6
7
8
9
I0
II
I2
I
2
3
4
5
6
7
8
9
I0
II
I2

ROOT

FLOWER

TEMPERATURE

MAX./MIN. _____ °F /°C

PRECIPITATION

CONDITIONS

WIND

N NE E SE S SW W NW

TEMPERATURE

MAX./MIN. _____ °F /°C

PRECIPITATION

CONDITIONS

WIND

N NE E SE S SW W NW

TEMPERATURE

MAX./MIN. _____ °F /°C

PRECIPITATION

CONDITIONS

WIND

N NE E SE S SW W NW

O B E R

THURSDAY 21   **FRIDAY 22**   **SATURDAY 23**

FLOWER

LEAF

1 2 3 4 5 6 7 8 9 10 11 12

TEMPERATURE

MAX./MIN._____°F/°C

PRECIPITATION

CONDITIONS

WIND

N NE E SE S SW W NW

SUNDAY 24

United Nations Day

LEAF

FRUIT

1 2 3 4 5 6 7 8 9 10 11 12 1 2 3 4 5 6 7 8 9 10 11 12

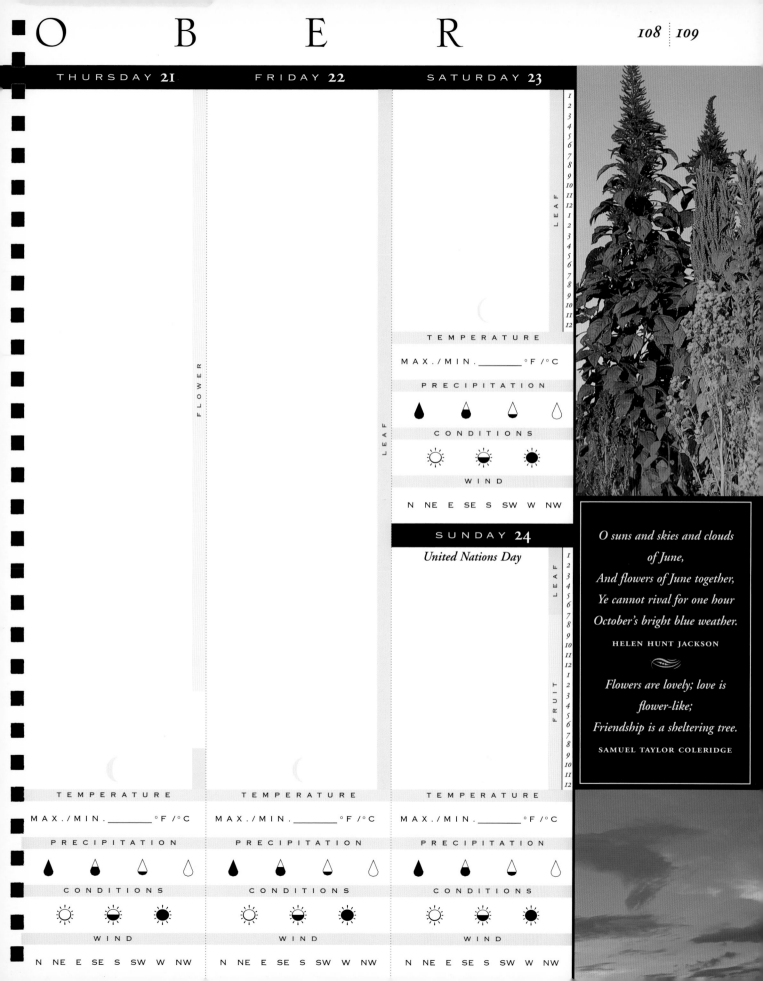

*O suns and skies and clouds
of June,
And flowers of June together,
Ye cannot rival for one hour
October's bright blue weather.*

HELEN HUNT JACKSON

*Flowers are lovely; love is
flower-like;
Friendship is a sheltering tree.*

SAMUEL TAYLOR COLERIDGE

TEMPERATURE

MAX./MIN._____°F/°C

PRECIPITATION

CONDITIONS

WIND

N NE E SE S SW W NW

TEMPERATURE

MAX./MIN._____°F/°C

PRECIPITATION

CONDITIONS

WIND

N NE E SE S SW W NW

TEMPERATURE

MAX./MIN._____°F/°C

PRECIPITATION

CONDITIONS

WIND

N NE E SE S SW W NW

MONDAY 25   **TUESDAY 26**   **WEDNESDAY 27**

*Feed your outdoor bulbs
with organic fertilizer
to replace nutrients in their soil
and mulch them.*

*Plant a tree!
Plant dormant trees now
through the early spring,
provided the soil is not too cold,
or frozen.
Water well, and through the
tree's first season.*

OCTOBER

M	T	W	T	F	S	S
				1	2	3
4	5	6	7	8	9	10
11	12	13	14	15	16	17
18	19	20	21	22	23	24
25	26	27	28	29	30	31

FRUIT

ROOT

ROOT

1 2 3 4 5 6 7 8 9 10 11 12 1 2 3 4 5 6 7 8 9 10 11 12

TEMPERATURE
MAX./MIN. _____ °F /°C
PRECIPITATION
CONDITIONS
WIND
N NE E SE S SW W NW

TEMPERATURE
MAX./MIN. _____ °F /°C
PRECIPITATION
CONDITIONS
WIND
N NE E SE S SW W NW

TEMPERATURE
MAX./MIN. _____ °F /°C
PRECIPITATION
CONDITIONS
WIND
N NE E SE S SW W NW

THURSDAY 28 · FRIDAY 29 · SATURDAY 30

SATURDAY 30

FLOWER

1 2 3 4 5 6 7 8 9 10 11 12 1 2 3 4 5 6 7 8 9 10 11 12

LEAF

TEMPERATURE

MAX./MIN. _____ °F /°C

PRECIPITATION

CONDITIONS

WIND

N NE E SE S SW W NW

SUNDAY 31

Daylight Saving Time Ends
Halloween

LEAF

1 2 3 4 5 6 7 8 9 10 11 12 1 2 3 4 5 6 7 8 9 10 11 12

LEAF

ROOT

FLOWER

FLOWER

TEMPERATURE

MAX./MIN. _____ °F /°C

PRECIPITATION

CONDITIONS

WIND

N NE E SE S SW W NW

TEMPERATURE

MAX./MIN. _____ °F /°C

PRECIPITATION

CONDITIONS

WIND

N NE E SE S SW W NW

TEMPERATURE

MAX./MIN. _____ °F /°C

PRECIPITATION

CONDITIONS

WIND

N NE E SE S SW W NW

> *There is something in October*
> *sets the gypsy blood astir.*
> WILLIAM BLISS CARMAN
>
> *No spring, nor summer*
> *beauty hath such grace,*
> *As I have seen in one*
> *autumnal face.*
> JOHN DONNE

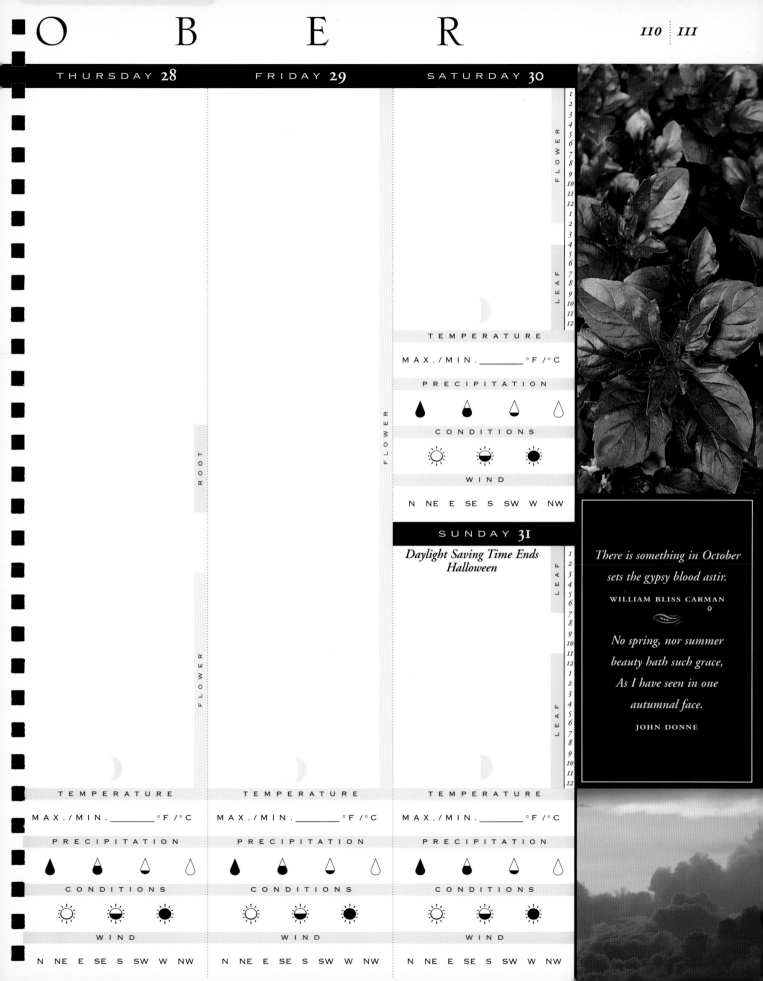

Dig or turn your soil now.
This will save valuable
time in the spring.

Apply compost to your soil.
Even if it is fibrous,
it will be ready by spring.

Mulch now so the soil
is protected from the harsh
winter elements and
holds in the moisture.

NOVEMBER

M	T	W	T	F	S	S
1	2	3	4	5	6	7
8	9	10	11	12	13	14
15	16	17	18	19	20	21
22	23	24	25	26	27	28
29	30					

I 2 3 4 5 6 7 8 9 10 11 12 I 2 3 4 5 6 7 8 9 10 11 12

MONDAY 1

All Saints' Day

FRUIT

TEMPERATURE

MAX./MIN. _____ °F /°C

PRECIPITATION

CONDITIONS

WIND

N NE E SE S SW W NW

TUESDAY 2

Election Day

FRUIT

TEMPERATURE

MAX./MIN. _____ °F /°C

PRECIPITATION

CONDITIONS

WIND

N NE E SE S SW W NW

WEDNESDAY 3

FRUIT

ROOT

TEMPERATURE

MAX./MIN. _____ °F /°C

PRECIPITATION

CONDITIONS

WIND

N NE E SE S SW W NW

THURSDAY 4	FRIDAY 5	SATURDAY 6

ROOT

ROOT

FRUIT

ROOT

1 2 3 4 5 6 7 8 9 10 11 12 1 2 3 4 5 6 7 8 9 10 11 12

TEMPERATURE

MAX./MIN. _____ °F /°C

PRECIPITATION

CONDITIONS

WIND

N NE E SE S SW W NW

SUNDAY 7

ROOT

FLOWER

1 2 3 4 5 6 7 8 9 10 11 12 1 2 3 4 5 6 7 8 9 10 11 12

TEMPERATURE	TEMPERATURE	TEMPERATURE
MAX./MIN. _____ °F /°C	MAX./MIN. _____ °F /°C	MAX./MIN. _____ °F /°C
PRECIPITATION	PRECIPITATION	PRECIPITATION
CONDITIONS	CONDITIONS	CONDITIONS
WIND	WIND	WIND
N NE E SE S SW W NW	N NE E SE S SW W NW	N NE E SE S SW W NW

*O, it sets my heart a-clickin'
like the tickin' of a clock,
When the frost is on the
punkin and the fodder's
in the shock.*

JAMES WHITCOMB RILEY

| MONDAY **8** | TUESDAY **9** | WEDNESDAY **10** |

Rake up and dispose of orchard leaves, mow, and remove mulch from tree trunks to discourage rodent habitat.

Prune your perennials.

Clean your tools and equipment carefully and repair them if necessary before storing them away for the winter.

NOVEMBER

M	T	W	T	F	S	S
I	2	3	4	5	6	7
8	9	IO	II	I2	I3	I4
I5	I6	I7	I8	I9	20	2I
22	23	24	25	26	27	28
29	30					

FLOWER

FLOWER

LEAF

ROOT

TEMPERATURE
MAX./MIN. _____ °F /°C

PRECIPITATION

CONDITIONS

WIND
N NE E SE S SW W NW

TEMPERATURE
MAX./MIN. _____ °F /°C

PRECIPITATION

CONDITIONS

WIND
N NE E SE S SW W NW

TEMPERATURE
MAX./MIN. _____ °F /°C

PRECIPITATION

CONDITIONS

WIND
N NE E SE S SW W NW

THURSDAY 11

Veterans Day
Remembrance Day (Canada)

LEAF

FRUIT

TEMPERATURE

MAX./MIN. _____ °F / °C

PRECIPITATION

CONDITIONS

WIND

N NE E SE S SW W NW

FRIDAY 12

SATURDAY 13

FRUIT

1
2
3
4
5
6
7
8
9
10
11
12

FRUIT

TEMPERATURE

MAX./MIN. _____ °F / °C

PRECIPITATION

CONDITIONS

WIND

N NE E SE S SW W NW

SUNDAY 14

ROOT

1
2
3
4
5
6
7
8
9
10
11
12
1
2
3
4
5
6
7
8
9
10
11
12

TEMPERATURE

MAX./MIN. _____ °F / °C

PRECIPITATION

CONDITIONS

WIND

N NE E SE S SW W NW

TEMPERATURE

MAX./MIN. _____ °F / °C

PRECIPITATION

CONDITIONS

WIND

N NE E SE S SW W NW

How many times it thundered before Franklin took the hint! How many apples fell on Newton's head before he took the hint! Nature is always hinting at us. It hints over and over again. And suddenly we take the hint.

ROBERT FROST

MONDAY 15   **TUESDAY 16**   **WEDNESDAY 17**

*Turn your inefficient lawn
into practical garden space.
Completely cover the grass
with black plastic
or cardboard and
wait a few weeks.
Then dig the dead
grass under and replant
with trees, shrubs, or prepare
growing beds.*

NOVEMBER

M	T	W	T	F	S	S
1	2	3	4	5	6	7
8	9	10	11	12	13	14
15	16	17	18	19	20	21
22	23	24	25	26	27	28
29	30					

ROOT   ROOT   FLOWER   FLOWER

1 2 3 4 5 6 7 8 9 10 11 12 1 2 3 4 5 6 7 8 9 10 11 12

TEMPERATURE   TEMPERATURE   TEMPERATURE

MAX./MIN. _____ °F /°C   MAX./MIN. _____ °F /°C   MAX./MIN. _____ °F /°C

PRECIPITATION   PRECIPITATION   PRECIPITATION

CONDITIONS   CONDITIONS   CONDITIONS

WIND   WIND   WIND

N NE E SE S SW W NW   N NE E SE S SW W NW   N NE E SE S SW W NW

THURSDAY 18 | FRIDAY 19 | SATURDAY 20

FLOWER

LEAF

ROOT

LEAF

1 2 3 4 5 6 7 8 9 10 11 12 1 2 3 4 5 6 7 8 9 10 11 12

TEMPERATURE

MAX./MIN. _____ °F /°C

PRECIPITATION

CONDITIONS

WIND

N NE E SE S SW W NW

SUNDAY 21

ROOT

FRUIT

1 2 3 4 5 6 7 8 9 10 11 12 1 2 3 4 5 6 7 8 9 10 11 12

TEMPERATURE

MAX./MIN. _____ °F /°C

PRECIPITATION

CONDITIONS

WIND

N NE E SE S SW W NW

TEMPERATURE

MAX./MIN. _____ °F /°C

PRECIPITATION

CONDITIONS

WIND

N NE E SE S SW W NW

TEMPERATURE

MAX./MIN. _____ °F /°C

PRECIPITATION

CONDITIONS

WIND

N NE E SE S SW W NW

*No warmth, no cheerfulness,
no healthful ease,
No comfortable feel in any
member –
No shade, no shine, no
butterflies, no bees,
No fruits, no flowers, no
leaves, no birds,
November!*

THOMAS HOOD

MONDAY 22

TUESDAY 23

WEDNESDAY 24

1
2
3
4
5
6
7
8
9
10
11
12
1
2
3
4
5
6
7
8
9
10
11
12

FRUIT

ROOT

ROOT

ROOT

> *It is the time*
> *for giving thanks*
> *for the garden harvest.*
>
> *Review your inventory*
> *of garden tools and develop*
> *a wish list. Drop hints about*
> *what you would like as*
> *a present in the forthcoming*
> *holiday season!*

NOVEMBER

M	T	W	T	F	S	S
1	2	3	4	5	6	7
8	9	10	11	12	13	14
15	16	17	18	19	20	21
22	23	24	25	26	27	28
29	30					

TEMPERATURE

MAX./MIN. _____ °F /°C

PRECIPITATION

CONDITIONS

WIND

N NE E SE S SW W NW

TEMPERATURE

MAX./MIN. _____ °F /°C

PRECIPITATION

CONDITIONS

WIND

N NE E SE S SW W NW

TEMPERATURE

MAX./MIN. _____ °F /°C

PRECIPITATION

CONDITIONS

WIND

N NE E SE S SW W NW

THURSDAY 25

Thanksgiving Day

FRIDAY 26

SATURDAY 27

LEAF

1
2
3
4
5
6
7
8
9
10
11
12

LEAF

1
2
3
4
5
6
7
8
9
10
11
12

FLOWER

TEMPERATURE

MAX./MIN. _____ °F /°C

PRECIPITATION

CONDITIONS

WIND

N NE E SE S SW W NW

SUNDAY 28

LEAF

1
2
3
4
5
6
7
8
9
10
11
12

FRUIT

1
2
3
4
5
6
7
8
9
10
11
12

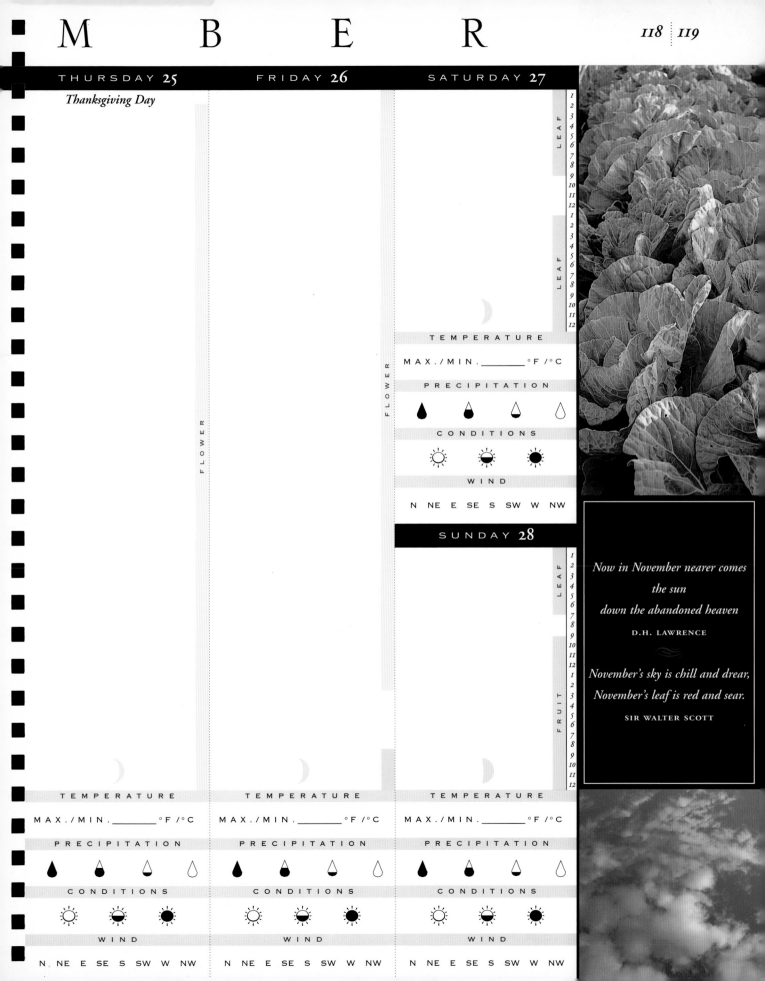

*Now in November nearer comes
the sun
down the abandoned heaven*

D.H. LAWRENCE

*November's sky is chill and drear,
November's leaf is red and sear.*

SIR WALTER SCOTT

TEMPERATURE

MAX./MIN. _____ °F /°C

PRECIPITATION

CONDITIONS

WIND

N NE E SE S SW W NW

TEMPERATURE

MAX./MIN. _____ °F /°C

PRECIPITATION

CONDITIONS

WIND

N NE E SE S SW W NW

TEMPERATURE

MAX./MIN. _____ °F /°C

PRECIPITATION

CONDITIONS

WIND

N NE E SE S SW W NW

MONDAY 29   **TUESDAY 30**   **WEDNESDAY 1**

Read a book about culinary
and medicinal herbs.
Learn about their
history and uses.
Plan to grow those herbs that
interest you most.

Maintain cloches and
cold frames to extend
your garden season
to the new year.

DECEMBER

M	T	W	T	F	S	S
		1	2	3	4	5
6	7	8	9	10	11	12
13	14	15	16	17	18	19
20	21	22	23	24	25	26
27	28	29	30	31		

1 2 3 4 5 6 7 8 9 10 11 12 1 2 3 4 5 6 7 8 9 10 11 12

FRUIT   FRUIT   ROOT

TEMPERATURE   TEMPERATURE   TEMPERATURE

MAX./MIN. _____ °F /°C   MAX./MIN. _____ °F /°C   MAX./MIN. _____ °F /°C

PRECIPITATION   PRECIPITATION   PRECIPITATION

CONDITIONS   CONDITIONS   CONDITIONS

WIND   WIND   WIND

N NE E SE S SW W NW   N NE E SE S SW W NW   N NE E SE S SW W NW

THURSDAY 2

FRIDAY 3

SATURDAY 4

Hanukkah

ROOT

1
2
3
4
5
6
7
8
9
10
11
12

FLOWER

1
2
3
4
5
6
7
8
9
10
11
12

ROOT

ROOT

TEMPERATURE

MAX. / MIN. _____ °F / °C

PRECIPITATION

CONDITIONS

WIND

N NE E SE S SW W NW

SUNDAY 5

FLOWER

1
2
3
4
5
6
7
8
9
10
11
12
1
2
3
4
5
6
7
8
9
10
11
12

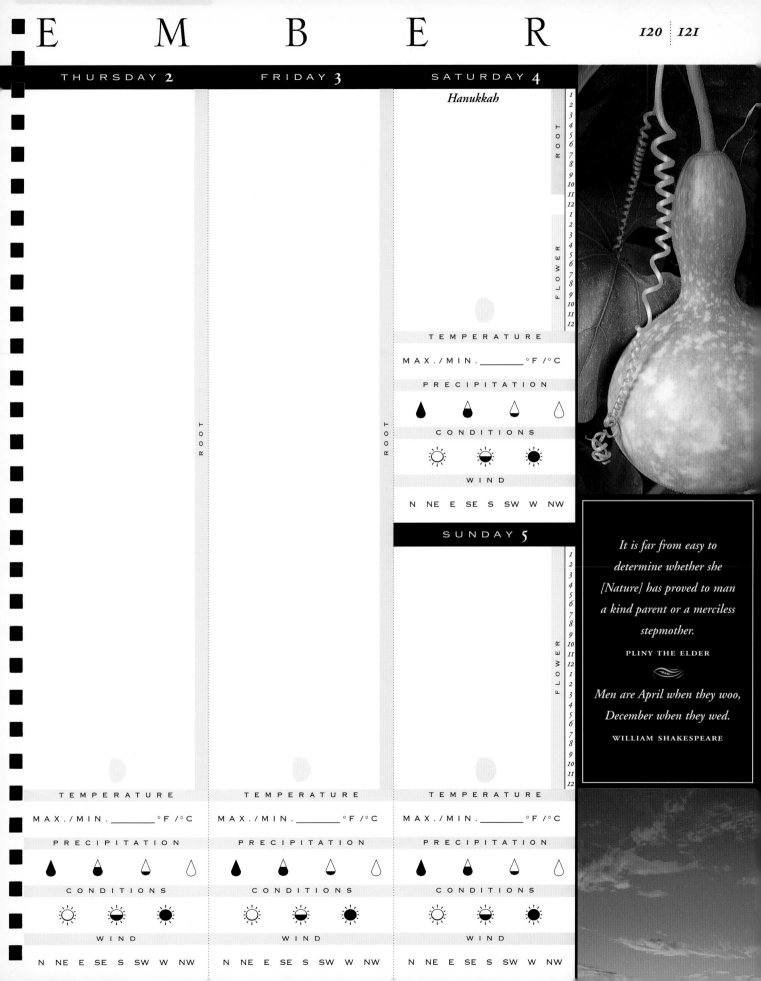

> *It is far from easy to determine whether she [Nature] has proved to man a kind parent or a merciless stepmother.*
>
> **PLINY THE ELDER**
>
> *Men are April when they woo, December when they wed.*
>
> **WILLIAM SHAKESPEARE**

TEMPERATURE

MAX. / MIN. _____ °F / °C

PRECIPITATION

CONDITIONS

WIND

N NE E SE S SW W NW

TEMPERATURE

MAX. / MIN. _____ °F / °C

PRECIPITATION

CONDITIONS

WIND

N NE E SE S SW W NW

TEMPERATURE

MAX. / MIN. _____ °F / °C

PRECIPITATION

CONDITIONS

WIND

N NE E SE S SW W NW

Order tree stock and seed;
picture beauty to be.
Remember the words of
Henry David Thoreau:
"I have great faith in a seed.
Convince me that you have
a seed there, and I am prepared
to expect wonders."

Apply white latex paint
to the trunks of your fruit trees
to prevent winter sunburn
and cracking.

DECEMBER

M	T	W	T	F	S	S
		1	2	3	4	5
6	7	8	9	10	11	12
13	14	15	16	17	18	19
20	21	22	23	24	25	26
27	28	29	30	31		

MONDAY 6

TUESDAY 7

WEDNESDAY 8

FLOWER

LEAF

LEAF

LEAF

FRUIT

TEMPERATURE

MAX. / MIN. _____ °F / °C

PRECIPITATION

CONDITIONS

WIND

N NE E SE S SW W NW

TEMPERATURE

MAX. / MIN. _____ °F / °C

PRECIPITATION

CONDITIONS

WIND

N NE E SE S SW W NW

TEMPERATURE

MAX. / MIN. _____ °F / °C

PRECIPITATION

CONDITIONS

WIND

N NE E SE S SW W NW

THURSDAY 9

FRIDAY 10

SATURDAY 11

FRUIT

ROOT

TEMPERATURE

MAX./MIN. _____ °F /°C

PRECIPITATION

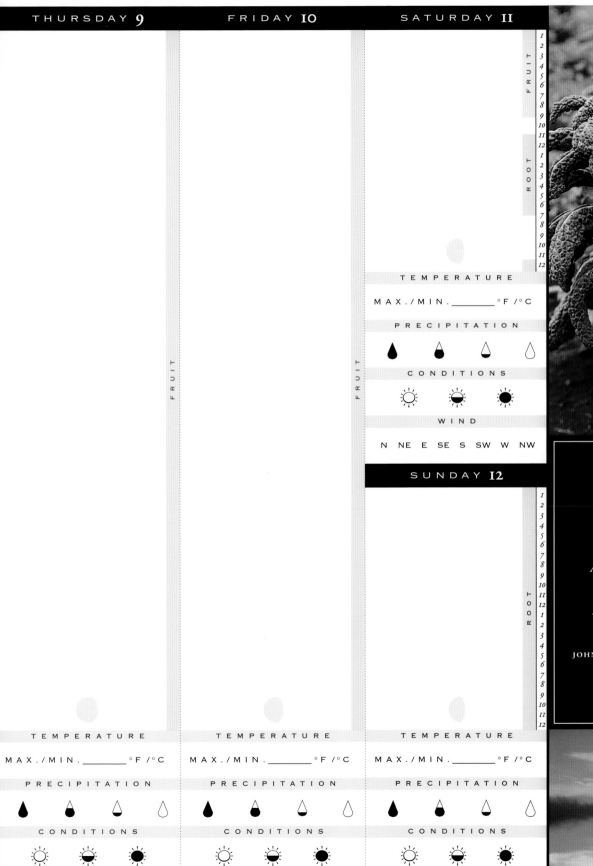

CONDITIONS

WIND

N NE E SE S SW W NW

SUNDAY 12

ROOT

FRUIT

*The sun that brief
December day
Rose cheerless over
hills of gray,
And, darkly, circled,
gave at noon
A sadder light than
the waning moon.*

JOHN GREENLEAF WHITTIER

TEMPERATURE

MAX./MIN. _____ °F /°C

PRECIPITATION

CONDITIONS

WIND

N NE E SE S SW W NW

TEMPERATURE

MAX./MIN. _____ °F /°C

PRECIPITATION

CONDITIONS

WIND

N NE E SE S SW W NW

TEMPERATURE

MAX./MIN. _____ °F /°C

PRECIPITATION

CONDITIONS

WIND

N NE E SE S SW W NW

Protect your compost
from the elements
until you are ready to use it
in the spring.

~

Review the gardening magazines
you are receiving and
check out those you aren't
at your local library
or bookstore.
Decide which ones to subscribe
to in the new year.

DECEMBER

M	T	W	T	F	S	S
		1	2	3	4	5
6	7	8	9	10	11	12
13	14	15	16	17	18	19
20	21	22	23	24	25	26
27	28	29	30	31		

MONDAY 13

TUESDAY 14

WEDNESDAY 15

ROOT

FLOWER

FLOWER

FLOWER

LEAF

1 2 3 4 5 6 7 8 9 10 11 12 1 2 3 4 5 6 7 8 9 10 11 12

TEMPERATURE

MAX./MIN. _____ °F /°C

PRECIPITATION

CONDITIONS

WIND

N NE E SE S SW W NW

TEMPERATURE

MAX./MIN. _____ °F /°C

PRECIPITATION

CONDITIONS

WIND

N NE E SE S SW W NW

TEMPERATURE

MAX./MIN. _____ °F /°C

PRECIPITATION

CONDITIONS

WIND

N NE E SE S SW W NW

THURSDAY 16 **FRIDAY 17** **SATURDAY 18**

LEAF

FRUIT

1 2 3 4 5 6 7 8 9 10 11 12
1 2 3 4 5 6 7 8 9 10 11 12

TEMPERATURE

MAX./MIN. _____ °F /°C

PRECIPITATION

CONDITIONS

WIND

N NE E SE S SW W NW

SUNDAY 19

LEAF

FRUIT

1 2 3 4 5 6 7 8 9 10 11 12
1 2 3 4 5 6 7 8 9 10 11 12

*Ah, distinctly, I remember
it was in the bleak
December;
And each separate dying
ember wrought its ghost
upon the floor.*

EDGAR ALLAN POE

TEMPERATURE

MAX./MIN. _____ °F /°C

PRECIPITATION

CONDITIONS

WIND

N NE E SE S SW W NW

TEMPERATURE

MAX./MIN. _____ °F /°C

PRECIPITATION

CONDITIONS

WIND

N NE E SE S SW W NW

TEMPERATURE

MAX./MIN. _____ °F /°C

PRECIPITATION

CONDITIONS

WIND

N NE E SE S SW W NW

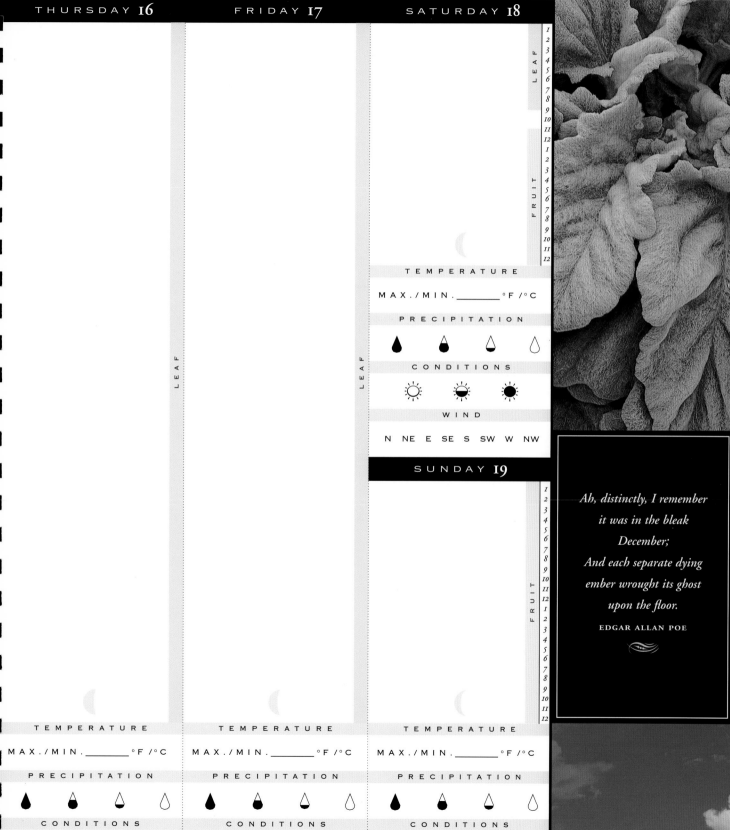

*If we had no winter,
the spring would not be so
pleasant: if we did not
sometimes taste of adversity,
prosperity would not be
so welcome.*

ANNE BRADSTREET,

"MEDITATIONS DIVINE AND MORAL"

MONDAY 20

TUESDAY 21

WEDNESDAY 22

Shortest Day of the Year:
Winter Begins

ROOT

ROOT

Prune your evergreens now –
and use the branches
for decoration in the home,
or mulch.

Enjoy time with your family
in the comfort of your home
during the holidays.
Reflect on your successes
in the garden during
the last year and the joy
of growing your own food,
flowers, and herbs.

DECEMBER

M	T	W	T	F	S	S
		1	2	3	4	5
6	7	8	9	10	11	12
13	14	15	16	17	18	19
20	21	22	23	24	25	26
27	28	29	30	31		

1
2
3
4
5
6
7
8
9
10
11
12
1
2
3
4
5
6
7
8
9
10
11
12

TEMPERATURE

MAX./MIN. _____ °F /°C

PRECIPITATION

CONDITIONS

WIND

N NE E SE S SW W NW

TEMPERATURE

MAX./MIN. _____ °F /°C

PRECIPITATION

CONDITIONS

WIND

N NE E SE S SW W NW

TEMPERATURE

MAX./MIN. _____ °F /°C

PRECIPITATION

CONDITIONS

WIND

N NE E SE S SW W NW

THURSDAY 23

FRIDAY 24

SATURDAY 25

Christmas Day

FLOWER

LEAF

FRUIT

1 2 3 4 5 6 7 8 9 10 11 12 1 2 3 4 5 6 7 8 9 10 11 12

TEMPERATURE

MAX./MIN. _____ °F /°C

PRECIPITATION

CONDITIONS

WIND

N NE E SE S SW W NW

SUNDAY 26

Boxing Day (Canada, UK)

LEAF

FRUIT

FLOWER

LEAF

1 2 3 4 5 6 7 8 9 10 11 12 1 2 3 4 5 6 7 8 9 10 11 12

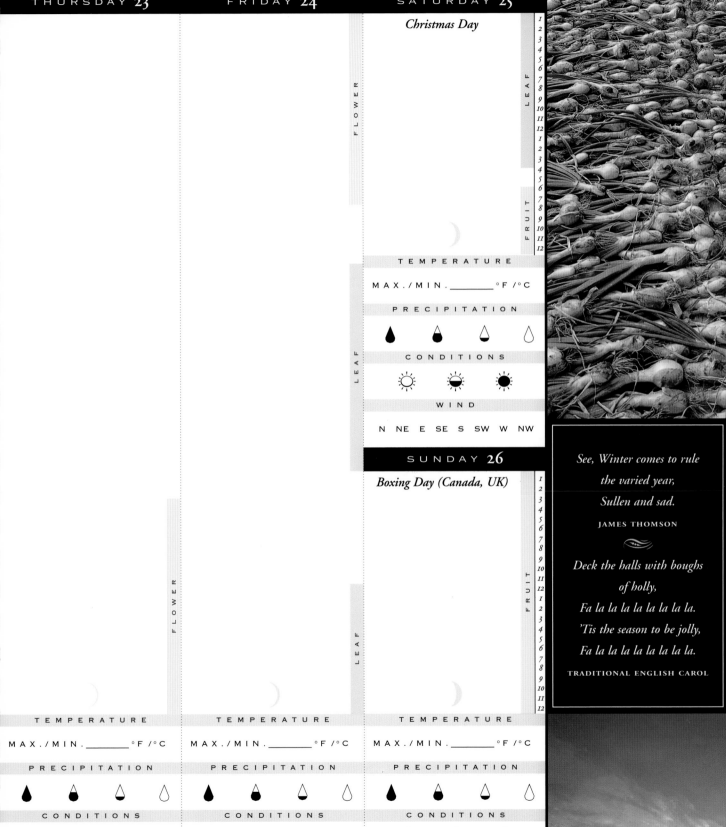

See, Winter comes to rule
the varied year,
Sullen and sad.

JAMES THOMSON

Deck the halls with boughs
of holly,
Fa la la la la la la la la.
'Tis the season to be jolly,
Fa la la la la la la la la.

TRADITIONAL ENGLISH CAROL

TEMPERATURE

MAX./MIN. _____ °F /°C

PRECIPITATION

CONDITIONS

WIND

N NE E SE S SW W NW

TEMPERATURE

MAX./MIN. _____ °F /°C

PRECIPITATION

CONDITIONS

WIND

N NE E SE S SW W NW

TEMPERATURE

MAX./MIN. _____ °F /°C

PRECIPITATION

CONDITIONS

WIND

N NE E SE S SW W NW

MONDAY 27   **TUESDAY 28**   **WEDNESDAY 29**

*Draw up a list of
New Year's resolutions
for the garden.
Keep this list in the front of
next year's GARDENCYCLE
and – most important of all –
stick to them!*

*Welcome in the new
millennium!*

LEAF   FRUIT   FRUIT   LEAF   ROOT   ROOT

1
2
3
4
5
6
7
8
9
10
11
12
1
2
3
4
5
6
7
8
9
10
11
12

DECEMBER

M	T	W	T	F	S	S
		1	2	3	4	5
6	7	8	9	10	11	12
13	14	15	16	17	18	19
20	21	22	23	24	25	26
27	28	29	30	31		

TEMPERATURE   TEMPERATURE   TEMPERATURE
MAX./MIN._____°F/°C   MAX./MIN._____°F/°C   MAX./MIN._____°F/°C
PRECIPITATION   PRECIPITATION   PRECIPITATION
CONDITIONS   CONDITIONS   CONDITIONS
WIND   WIND   WIND
N NE E SE S SW W NW   N NE E SE S SW W NW   N NE E SE S SW W NW

THURSDAY 30

FRIDAY 31

SATURDAY 1

New Year's Day

ROOT

ROOT

FLOWER

1 2 3 4 5 6 7 8 9 10 11 12 1 2 3 4 5 6 7 8 9 10 11 12

TEMPERATURE

MAX./MIN. _____ °F /°C

PRECIPITATION

CONDITIONS

WIND

N NE E SE S SW W NW

SUNDAY 2

1 2 3 4 5 6 7 8 9 10 11 12 1 2 3 4 5 6 7 8 9 10 11 12

We are stardust,
We are golden,
And we've got to get ourselves
Back to the garden.

JONI MITCHELL

TEMPERATURE

MAX./MIN. _____ °F /°C

PRECIPITATION

CONDITIONS

WIND

N NE E SE S SW W NW

TEMPERATURE

MAX./MIN. _____ °F /°C

PRECIPITATION

CONDITIONS

WIND

N NE E SE S SW W NW

TEMPERATURE

MAX./MIN. _____ °F /°C

PRECIPITATION

CONDITIONS

WIND

N NE E SE S SW W. NW

At least six million American households are actively engaged in composting their own kitchen and garden waste, and the trend is rapidly rising. Even in urban areas, kitchen scraps can be composted in a small backyard, or taken to a compost center or community garden. Managing compost is simple and rewarding, and it takes only a few minutes per week. Whether occurring naturally or man-made, composting is the most efficient means of building humus and thus soil.

THE DYNAMICS OF COMPOSTING

Composting requires the presence of both air and water, so microorganisms can breathe and take in moisture. Too much of either is detrimental to the process of decomposition, but a damp, aerated compost pile is ideal. Materials should be added in such as way that there are pockets of air, but not arranged so loosely that there is too much. The time for composting to be completed will vary greatly depending on the volume of compost, the climate, moisture, and the types of materials used. The average time to allow for the process to cycle is three to six months. In planning ahead, bear in mind that compost is most effectively used in the spring, when preparing the soil for planting.

The three essential components of compost are green vegetation, brown vegetation, and soil. These components can be added in even proportions. Green vegetation provides nitrogen for the microorganisms that break the compost down. Green ingredients include fresh grass clippings, recently pulled weeds, leaves, flowers, kelp, and kitchen scraps. Appropriate kitchen scraps include fruit skins, peels and cores, vegetable parts, tea leaves, coffee grounds, stale bread, and nonmeat left-overs. Brown (or dry) vegetation provides carbon, a vital food source for microorganisms. These materials include dry (old) grass clippings, weeds, leaves and flowers, woody stems, straw, paper towels, and wood chips. A significant portion of the brown vegetation should be watered so that it breaks down more easily. Good quality top soil with active microorganisms accelerates the decomposition while keeping it stable. These microorganisms break down complex compounds in the compost into a form that plants can assimilate. These compounds also contain antibiotics, vitamins, and enzymes that protect plants from disease. Adding soil also helps retain moisture and minimize odors.

Keep pets away from the compost. Manure from meat-eating animals such as dogs and cats may contain disease-producing organisms. Certain other items should be added with caution. Weeds and disease- or pest-affected plants should only be added to "hot" piles that are decomposing rapidly (with an internal temperature of at least 130 degrees F.). Pernicious plants and thick or fibrous material are best chopped up and dried, or alternatively burned, before being added. Poisonous plants such as hemlock and castor, and acidic or toxin-bearing tree leaves such as bay laurel, eucalyptus, juniper, pine, and walnut, can disrupt and distress the soil organisms and should be added sparingly, if at all.

COMPOSTING TECHNIQUES

Start by choosing a location that is conveniently placed for access from the kitchen (for waste disposal), to water, in case extra moisture is needed, and to the garden site where the compost will eventually be needed. Compost can be collected free-form, in a pile, or con-

fined tidily in a bin, barrel, or frame. There are a number of wire, wood, or plastic containers on the market, or you can make your own. With smaller quantities of compost, it is also possible to use the "pit" method (or sheet composting), which involves digging a hole in the ground to a depth of about a foot. The organic matter should be combined with at least eight inches of soil and buried in the ground.

If compost is piled, place it on soil, not a paved surface, and avoid siting it next to a fence or building which in time will begin to rot. Allow for adequate drainage. Layer the compost as you would a lasagna, starting with a two-inch layer of brown (dry) vegetation, an equal amount of green vegetation, and then a layer of soil. Layering your compost in approximately equal proportions will provide an ideal carbon-nitrogen ratio. After adding each layer, water lightly to keep the compost evenly moist; too much water will drown the microorganisms, and too little will decrease activity. Layering compost requires significant amounts of brown and green vegetation at a time; if you generate only small quantities of such material, building a compost pile spontaneously as waste becomes available will also work, although it may take longer to cure.

It is most desirable to balance the components of compost, as adding too much green vegetation will cause the decomposition process to move rapidly, producing unpleasant odors, while too much brown vegetation will impede the decomposition process, preventing the compost from becoming warm enough. However, some gardeners and farmers such as Dr. Howard-Yana Shapiro, Director of Agriculture for Seeds of Change, prefer using cold compost piles that decompose more slowly through the action of anaerobic bacteria. These piles are composed mainly of dense brown vegetation, and the higher levels of carbon produced in the humus boost soil fertility.

There are several indicators that the composting process is complete and that the compost is cured and ready to use. The original components of the compost should be unrecognizable; the mixture should be an even dark brown or black in color, with a fine, crumbly texture; there should be an absence of any heat in the compost; and there should be a woodsy smell, like a rich soil – sweet, with no aroma of decomposition. Do not let cured compost sit for too long, as it will continue to evolve from humus into topsoil, and its nutrients will be lost. If you cannot use it straight away, cover it with plastic to protect it from the elements and to keep its moisture enclosed.

SPECIFIC PLANT RECOMMENDATIONS FOR GROWING COMPOST

Master gardener John Jeavons, among others, suggests that to attain sustainable soil fertility, you should consider growing certain crops not only for food, but for the nutrient value they provide when composted. Such crops include fava beans, vetch, wheat, clover, agricultural mustard, oats, and rye. In milder climates, these crops can be grown during the winter. All of these cover crops fix nitrogen in the soil, further improving its quality (an important advantage for growing tomatoes and corn especially, which need large amounts of nitrogen), as well as providing nitrogen for composting.

THE CHADWICK TOMATO, NAMED AFTER ALAN CHADWICK.

This profile highlights the life and work of Alan Chadwick, whose inspirational teaching and accomplishments accelerated the acceptance of sustainable organic backyard gardening by a wide audience. Chadwick influenced a generation of gardeners, including the staff at Seeds of Change.

Alan Chadwick was a brilliant master gardener, a visionary, and an extraordinary source of inspiration for many horticulture students and professional gardeners, past and present. Through those who worked with him, and the constant stream of luminaries, writers, practitioners, and students who visited his magical gardens, Chadwick influenced an entire generation of American gardeners, whether directly or indirectly. In his fertile, productive gardens, Chadwick proved that by following his methods, yields of four to six times the U.S. commercial average for fruits, vegetables, and grains could be achieved, using one-eighth of the water, a quarter of the fertilizer, and one-hundredth of the energy per pound of food produced.

To Chadwick, gardening was in part a spiritual endeavor: an element in the quest for the inner sense of man, a means of shedding light on a vision of creation and nature. He was fascinated by the mystery of nature and the power of its cycles; he saw nature essentially as a giver and forgiver, and he battled constantly to defend it against man's predilection for dominating it. Chadwick saw the garden as our true home and as the ultimate teacher of human culture, and he strove to make his gardens as beautiful, functional, and sustainable as possible.

Alan Chadwick was born into an aristocratic English family in 1909 and trained as a Shakespearean actor. Later, he turned to gardening, although the reasons for this transition have never been clear (indeed, relatively little has been written about Chadwick because the facts were always difficult to establish). Perhaps his upbringing in a well-to-do family (for whom gardening was considered an art form) set him on this path. Through his mother's interests in the Anthroposophical Society, Chadwick was strongly influenced early on by the biodynamic theories of the Austrian philosopher, Rudolf Steiner, and also the French Intensive method of gardening popularized in France in the 1890s. From these main foundations, Alan developed the methods that he would teach to his students: double digging the soil, creating raised beds, using organic fertilizer and rejecting the use of chemicals in any form, sophisticated composting, employing companion planting and beneficial natural predators for pest control.

Chadwick moved to California in the early 1970s when he was invited by the University of California at Santa Cruz to establish a student garden and training program to demonstrate his methods. Dr. Paul Lee, Founder of the UCSC student garden project remembers Chadwick as "tall and handsome, a huge shock of hair, theatrical in demeanor, balletic in bearing." Alan York, past President of the Bio-Dynamic Farming and Gardening Association and orchard keeper, moved from Louisiana to California in the late 1960s and took up a career in gardening. "My life was full, and really good," York recalls. "Then I met this absolute wild man named Alan Chadwick who was growing incredible crops and flowers. He was gardening biodynamically and teaching a bunch of us young people about the philosophy of Rudolf Steiner in his totally unique style. I realized then that I had fallen in love for the first time with growing plants." York worked with Chadwick for three years in the mid-1970s as Head Gardener of the Round Valley Institute for the Study of Man and Nature at Covelo, California, executing Chadwick's directions, managing every detail of the spectacular garden, and supervising a staff of enthusiastic young gardeners.

Hilmar Moore, another former President of the Bio-Dynamic Farming and Gardening Association and an educator who also worked directly with Chadwick, echoes York's experience: "Soon, his incredibly beautiful and productive garden, his inspirational lectures, and his magnetic personality had attracted a devoted group of gardeners." Chadwick also helped develop several other productive gardens in California

and Virginia. "His vividly pictorial lectures on the management of fertilization, propagation, irrigation, and cultivation within the cycle of the year, the breathing of the earth, will live as long as people remember his words," recalls Moore.

"Organic gardening before Alan Chadwick was a series of hits and misses: try this, and when it doesn't work, try that," says York. "It was one garden tip after another. It was a time when chemical pesticides, herbicides, and fertilizers reigned supreme. Back in Louisiana, I remember DDT being sprayed all over the subdivision we lived in to keep the mosquitoes down. No one questioned anything, and it was an era of better living through chemistry. There was probably no better time for Alan Chadwick to arrive in the United States; there was a whole generation completely disillusioned with the way things were done and who were looking for something that had meaning. This was the generation that turned to counterculture, and when it became apparent that this was not sustainable either, for many it was 'back to the land.'"

York describes the impact that Chadwick made on his gardens and those around him: "Order! All of a sudden, there was order and discipline, and a defined and systematic methodology. Chadwick taught organized methods in his impassioned lectures, and they worked—not just now and then but every time. Chadwick's methodology involved a marriage of the universal principles of classical horticulture with organic gardening. What we all learned, working for him, was that when the discipline of order was followed, the results were spectacular."

"Alan Chadwick's gift, I believe, was not so much as a gardener as a storyteller. His storytelling was so skillful that he could create magic with words. This magic allowed those who worked with him to experience things that were still in the future, such as the building of a garden. Weaving his spell, Chadwick created vivid pictures that empowered us to visualize just what a garden could be. He always told us that it is the garden that makes the gardener, and not the other way around. It should be a place of reflection, he would say, where we can once again know that feeling of Paradise and recreate a modern Garden of Eden."

"For those who were fortunate enough to know him," concludes York, "his legacy will always live on because he captured our imaginations and gave us practical skills to turn our dreams into the reality of our lives."

1. SEED COMPANIES

Seeds of Change
Certified Organic
PO Box 15700
Santa Fe, NM 87506-5700
Telephone: (888)762-7333 *(toll free)*
Facsimile: (888)329-4762 *(toll free)*
E-mail:
gardner@seedsofchange.com
www.seedsofchange.com

Deep Diversity
A Planetary Gene Pool Resource
PO Box 15700
Santa Fe, NM 87506-5700
(Contact by mail only)

Abundant Life
PO Box 772
1029 Lawrence Street
Port Townsend, WA 98368
Telephone: (360) 385-5660
Facsimile: (360) 385-7455

Bountiful Gardens
18001 Shafer Ranch Road
Willits, CA 95490-9626
Telephone: (707) 459-6410

Elixir Farm Botanicals
(Medicinal Plant Seeds)
Brixey, MO 65618
Telephone: (417) 261-2393

Garden City Seeds
778 Hwy 93N
Hamilton, MT 59840-9448
Telephone: (406) 961-4837
Facsimile: (406) 961-4877

J.L. Hudson, Seedsman
Star Route 2, Box 337
La Honda, CA 94929
(Contact by phone only)

Native Seeds/Search
526 North 4th Avenue
Tucson, AZ 85705
Telephone: (520) 622-5561
Facsimile: (520) 622-5591

Prairie Moon Nursery
Route 3, Box 163
Winona, MN 55987-9515
Telephone: (507) 452-1362
Facsimile: (507) 454-5238

Seed Savers Exchange
3076 North Winn Road
Decorah, IA 52101
Telephone: (319) 382-5990

Synergy Seeds
PO Box 787
Somes Bar, CA 95568
Telephone: (916) 321-3769

2. RARE FRUIT TREES

Exotica Rare Fruit Nursery
PO Box 160
Vista, CA 92085
Telephone: (619) 724-9093

Sonoma Antique Apple Nursery
4395 Westside Road
Healdsburg, CA 95448
Telephone: (707) 433-6420

Southmeadow Fruit Farms
Box SM
Lakeside, MI 49116
Telephone: (616) 469-2865

3. INTERESTING TREES & PLANTS

Forest Farm
990 Tetherow Raod
Williams, OR 97544-9599
Telephone: (541) 846-7269
Facsimile: (541) 846-6963

Glasshouse Works
Church Street
Stewart, OH 45778-0097
Telephone: (614) 662-2142

Logee's Greenhouses
141 North Street
Danielson, CT 06239
Telephone: (203) 774-8038
Facsimile: (203) 774-9932

Mesa Garden
PO Box 72
Belen, NM 87002
Telephone: (505) 864-3131
Facsimile: (505) 864-3124

Northern Groves Bamboo
PO Box 86291
Portland, OR 97286-0291
Telephone: (503) 774-6353

Plants of the Southwest
Agua Fria, Rt. 6, Box 11A
Santa Fe, NM 87505
Telephone: (505) 471-2212

Rare Conifer Nursery
PO Box 100
Potter Valley, CA 95469
Facsimile: (707) 462-9536
(Contact by mail or fax only)

4. ORGANIZATIONS

The Bio-Dynamic Farming and
Gardening Association, Inc.
Bldg. 1002B, Thoreau Center,
The Presido
PO Box 29135
San Francisco, CA 94129-0135
Telephone: (415) 561-7797
Facsimile: (415) 561-7796
E-mail: Biodynamic@aol.com

Ecology Action
Sustainable Biointensive
Mini-Farming
5798 Ridgewood Road
Willits, CA 95490
Telephone: (707) 459-0150
Facsimile: (707) 459-5409

The Land Institute
2440 Water Well Road
Salina, KS 67401
Telephone: (913) 823-5376
Facsimile: (913) 823-8728

The Permaculture Institute
PO Box 3702
Pojoaque, NM 87501
(Contact by mail only)

5. OTHER

There are a large number of
societies dedicated to almost
every type of popular plant or
tree. For information and
further sources, contact your
local botanical garden or
agricultural extension agent.
Alternatively, check the Internet.

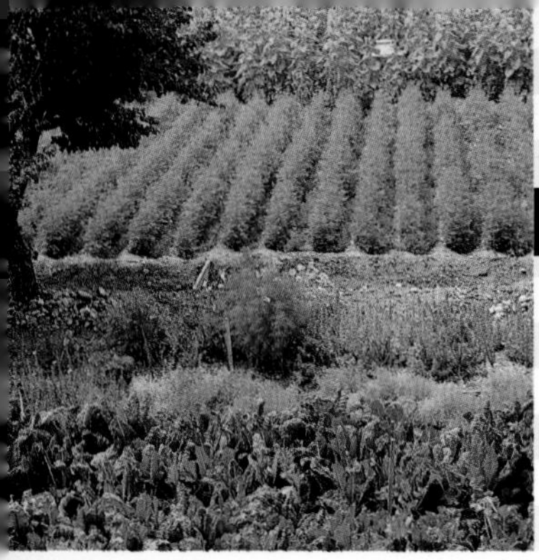

N O

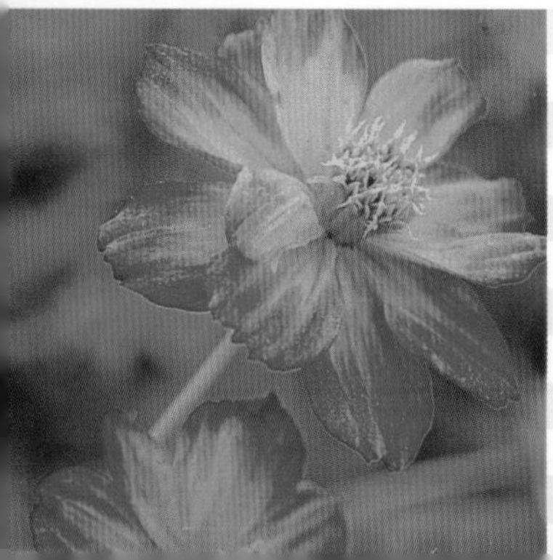